THE HEALTHY SELFIE

DR SUSIE DAVIES

The information provided in *The Healthy Selfie* is intended for general informational and educational purposes only. While the author, Dr Susie Davies, is a qualified mental health professional, the content of this book is not intended to replace personalised medical advice, diagnosis, or treatment. The material presented here should not be used as a substitute for seeking appropriate professional care for mental health issues. If you or someone you know is experiencing a mental health crisis, please seek immediate help from a qualified healthcare provider, therapist, or emergency services.

Any references to patients in this book are fictional and are not representative of any real individuals. Any resemblance to actual persons, living or deceased, is purely coincidental.

Always consult with a qualified healthcare provider or mental health professional before making any changes to your treatment plan or starting any new mental health regimen. The author and publisher disclaim any liability for any adverse effects arising from the use or application of the information contained in this book.

It is not guaranteed that URLs or websites mentioned in this publication will remain accurate or accessible over time. While every effort has been made to ensure accuracy, the publisher apologises for any errors or omissions in the copyright material. We would be grateful if notified of any corrections, which will be incorporated into future editions of this book.

Agency photographs: cover background and p4 background courtesy of Unsplash.com

ISBN: 978-1-0687950-0-8

First Edition

**TO HUGH, ISABELLE,
BETH AND THEO**

You are my everything.

CONTENTS

Introduction		06
1	It's hard to be happy if you don't like yourself	10
2	Cultivating self-acceptance	22
3	Building self-esteem	36
4	Stop comparing yourself to others	58
5	You are what you think	66
6	Growing your mindset	90
7	Bouncing back when things go wrong	112
8	Real relationships	126
9	Understanding stress	138
10	Wellness	154
11	The impact of screen time on your health	178
Conclusion		206
Appendix: Internet safety		208
Resources		216

INTRODUCTION

THE COMPUTER IN OUR POCKET

Smartphones, social media and new technology are an integral part of all of our lives. The smartphone is literally a computer in our pockets. It connects us with the world, entertains us; it's our camera, news source, library, bank, stereo, watch, fitness coach, map, bus ticket, travel agent, companion and so much more. The list is endless. And it's hard to remember that even a few years ago all these activities required their own devices, or even a trip out to the bank or library. You may consider in disbelief queueing at a ticket office or buying CDs from a music store to play on a huge ghetto blaster. However, the impact of this small square of silicone isn't just convenience.

Consider for a moment the different spheres of your life: your friends, family, education, values, hopes and dreams, what you eat, even how you think. I wonder if there's a single area where technology doesn't influence your choices. In this book, I'll help you to explore your life through the lens of technology (especially social media) and see how its influence weaves through your thoughts, feelings, behaviours and, ultimately, your happiness. Over the next 11 chapters, I'll help you to consider the impact of technology on your well-being and to make choices that enable you to be your happiest, healthiest self.

Since the invention of the smartphone, the selfie has boomed in popularity, so much so that 'selfie' was the Oxford Dictionaries' word of the year in 2013. It's become so ingrained in how we behave that it's almost a subconscious part of our lives. Many of us take and post multiple photos on our smartphones every day, including photos of ourselves. We also scroll past hundreds of other people's perfected selfies on social media, often pictures of influencers or celebrities we follow. With such a rapid change in culture, it makes sense to pause and reflect on the impact that this behaviour has on us and how we feel about ourselves.

The title of this book, *The Healthy Selfie*, isn't just a play on words. It's about the impact of the selfie on us, the unrealistic standards they can set and the effect on our self-image. Posting a selfie may seem like a benign action, but there can be many consequences - for example, other people's responses (or lack thereof) can affect how we feel about ourselves, and the online image we portray can shape how people view us. In fact, posting a selfie has been shown to make us feel more anxious and less attractive, and lower our mood. [1]

WHAT IS A HEALTHY SELFIE?

I wonder what images come to mind when you think of a *healthy* selfie? Do you think of yourself, or do you think of someone else's *healthy* post? Your first impression of a healthy selfie may be of someone who's physically fit or has adopted a clean-living lifestyle. Perhaps you're thinking of an influencer posing at the gym or someone with spot-free skin and glowing hair. Or maybe you're imagining someone who posts selfies of themselves enjoying the outdoors, or a person who shares snaps in which they're beaming and happy. Or, to you, does a healthy selfie mean popularity online or being a successful influencer? Do you subconsciously try to portray some or all of these attributes in your selfies?

How often do you post a selfie online? Or more importantly, how often do you like the image of yourself that you see? How often do you retake (multiple times), add filters, and change the lighting and the backdrop?

You may prefer the enhanced image, but is that image really you? Or to ask a more profound question, do you like the person behind the photo?

Unfortunately, altering the outside can't change how you feel about yourself on the inside. First, you need to change how you *think* about yourself, and then how you *feel* about yourself will improve. Whilst all the external things (like a fitness regime and healthy eating) are important, I want to help you explore real health on an emotional and physical level. Although the selfie is a two-dimensional reflection, it represents something much more poignant - how we feel about ourselves, and this is what I want to help you explore and, if necessary, repair.

> The healthy selfie is about being happy with ourselves on the inside and out. It's not just about looking good or wholesome eating habits.

This book is about how you can have a healthier view of yourself. It might seem a daunting or impossible task, but you can learn to be free from self-doubt and self-dislike. I've written this book for anyone who wants to understand the role that technology has in their life or is curious as to why they are feeling unhappy (especially with themselves). This book is for anyone who recognises they don't like themselves and wants to improve their self-esteem. It's also for anyone who recognises (or is being advised) that they have an unhealthy relationship with their phone. I hope that reading this book will help you to have a better understanding of yourself, the invisible impact of technology and what you can do to believe in yourself more. It's intended to help you evaluate your relationship with social media and how you can use it in a way that benefits you. The complex picture of adolescence and young adulthood has changed dramatically since my teenage years, and social media has changed the landscape indelibly. However, the same issues of self-esteem and self-acceptance are still at the forefront for teenagers, although they're now magnified by the lens of your phone and the social media platforms you post on.

CHANGE IS POSSIBLE

I work as a GP in Bristol. I have two teenage daughters, so this topic is very important to me. I've spoken to hundreds of patients in my consulting room and listened to their stories. Every day, I see people struggling with their mental health. Often, I can trace the underlying issue to low self-esteem that's driven by comparing themselves to others on social media. I have, over time, helped many of these people feel better about themselves. I run a charity called PAPAYA, which runs workshops for young people, helping them build their self-esteem and manage their relationship with social media. Many students have shared with me their personal journey with technology and the impact it has on their mental health. I've written this book to bring together everything I've learnt from my patients, the hundreds of teenagers who've come along to the workshops, and the reading and research I've done on self-esteem and social media.

Whoever you are and whatever your life looks like, you're worth believing in. You don't have to be the best or the most beautiful, or have the most followers, to be liked and lovable. There's no point spending your whole life, or even one more day, feeling down about yourself. It won't make you happy or make the world a better place. Feeling like a failure, being self-critical and comparing yourself negatively with others won't help. The journey to your healthier self begins as you accept your imperfections and start to believe in yourself. It doesn't happen overnight, but it starts with a desire to change how you feel about yourself. This book aims to equip you with the tools to make those changes. Even the thought of this may seem impossible, and it may tempt you to put this book down before you've even begun. Maybe my younger self would have done just that. However, change is possible, and why wait until you're 40 to discover that? You can transform how you feel by changing your self-view and learning to recognise and replace negative self-talk. So as a first step, read on! Don't give up on yourself and don't believe the lies in your head that you're not worth it or will never feel better. Change is more than possible.

This book has 11 chapters. They look at different areas of your life that can impact your health and happiness, especially the role of social media in your well-being. The first half of the book looks at how you view yourself and the impact other people's posts have on you, while the second half looks at how you can develop healthy habits and a balanced lifestyle. Each chapter includes some exercises at the end that you can work on in your own time. I suggest finding a restful, quiet space to read. Maybe turn your phone off or put it on silent! Spend some time focusing on you. If you want to do the exercises separately rather than in the book itself (or you're reading this online), a pen and notepad will be helpful. You may be very busy, but please give yourself a little time to look after yourself. Learn to enjoy your own company and discover your healthy selfie.

CHAPTER 1

IT'S HARD TO BE HAPPY IF YOU DON'T LIKE YOURSELF

Neave was an incredibly beautiful 18-year-old. Strangers regularly stopped her in the street to compliment her and she never had to pay for a drink. Online, she had hundreds of followers who adored her posts and selfies. However, despite all the positive affirmation she received, she didn't believe she was beautiful and struggled to accept herself. She didn't like how she looked and confided to me that she felt overweight and ugly. Despite doing well academically, she was convinced she was a failure and not good enough. She felt deeply unhappy.

To regain a sense of control, Neave had started reducing her calorie intake. She began skipping meals and lying about her eating to her friends and family. Neave was already very slim, so it wasn't long before she became dangerously underweight. Eventually, she was diagnosed with anorexia and had to take significant time out of school. During the next few months, she went through intensive therapy.

It was several years before I saw Neave again. She looked happier, healthier and brighter. I asked her what had changed and she replied, 'I learned to like myself.' I have never forgotten those words.

HOW CAN WE BE HAPPY?

Let's begin with a *big* question – how can we be happy? Really, this is a trick question, as in many ways it's an impossible one to answer. However, if we do want to try to answer one of life's biggest questions, we first need to think about what happiness is.

Interestingly, we put a lot of pressure on ourselves to 'be happy'. Our *true* desire may be for long-term happiness and contentment, but what we *crave* (and are sold through powerful advertising) is hedonistic happiness: the buzz of fun and pleasure and the absence of pain. This explains why the pursuit of happiness is a billion-pound industry (think smoking, alcohol, gambling, entertainment, social media, gaming and even sex and dating sites). The marketing world sells us hundreds of ways to find 'happiness', but in fact what most of us actually want isn't the 'quick fix' but a longer-term sense of purpose and belonging.

Longer-term happiness is harder to find and we often substitute it with easier happiness-inducing activities. It may be no surprise to you that repeatedly filling up on these quick fixes (whether it be scrolling on Instagram, posting a video on TikTok, vaping or overreliance on alcohol) doesn't actually result in long-term happiness. In fact, it can create quite the opposite: a loss of purpose and overdependence on these feel-good activities. Over time you even begin to feel less good as you need more of the happiness-inducing activity to get the same response (something called tolerance).

As we look at the healthy selfie, I want to help you explore how you can find longer-term contentment and happiness by changing how you *feel* about yourself. Liking ourselves is fundamental to our happiness and contentment. [2] Put simply, **to be happy, we need to like ourselves**. It gives us the confidence to believe in ourselves and to keep going when things are difficult, and it enables us to make good life choices and invest in positive relationships. Therefore, we're going to start by exploring how you can learn to like yourself more, and how this can help make you happier (or at least more content).

Notice the wording – to be happy, you need to like yourself. It doesn't matter how many other people like you (either digitally or in real life); you need to like yourself. In today's digital age it's so easy to look to others for your opinion of yourself. You may defer simple decisions to the online world (what to wear on a night out or where to eat), but on a far more meaningful level you can also defer how you feel about yourself to *like* counts and comments. Consider that again – it doesn't matter how many other people like you; you need to like yourself!

Whether or not you like yourself may not be something you've ever considered before. Self-dislike can be hidden by many labels and circumstances, but if present, it will negatively impact how you think about yourself. This in turn will influence your behaviour and how you treat yourself.

There are many reasons you may find it hard to like and accept yourself. It may be that you've been criticised or bullied and have taken these comments to heart. Or perhaps some tough things have happened to you during your life that are still very painful and difficult for you. Maybe you've lost a parent either through bereavement or family breakdown, you've been abused or your home life is very challenging. It can be hard to feel positive about yourself if you've been through, or are going through, a complicated or traumatic childhood.

However, many people won't have experienced any significant trauma, and yet they can still struggle to like and accept themselves. Being happy and having good mental health appears to be getting harder for everyone, especially young people. So whether you've experienced significant trauma or not, it's worth considering whether social media and our online world are having an impact on your ability to like yourself and therefore feel happy.

LIKING YOURSELF

Our ability to like ourselves isn't a matter of chance; it's determined by the interplay between our level of **self-acceptance** and **self-esteem**.

Liking yourself = self-acceptance + self-esteem

Self-acceptance and self-esteem may sound like the same thing, but there's a subtle difference between the two. Self-acceptance is our ability to *accept* ourselves as we are here and now, which includes accepting our faults and inevitable failures. Self-esteem is our *evaluation* of who we really are (it's how we see ourselves). Both are key to our happiness!

You may believe that other people liking and accepting you is more important than you liking and accepting yourself, but this isn't true. Feeling that other people like you can make you feel better temporarily; and in today's digital world often the easiest place to look for validation is your social media accounts. However, no number of social media *likes* can make you feel truly loved and accepted. If instead you like yourself, you don't need to wait for or rely on other people, as you can be your own reliable and constant encourager. The only opinion that really counts is your own – liking yourself can only really come from inside of you. Likes from other people (especially

Our ability to like ourselves isn’t a matter of chance; it’s determined by the interplay between our level of self-acceptance and self-esteem.

digital ones) are like sticking a plaster on a cut. It makes the cut less painful, but only your body can heal it. If you keep putting bandages on, you can actually prevent the cut from healing. Like the plaster, other people's likes can make you feel better. However, you can only find true healing and acceptance on the inside.

SELF-TALK

Have you ever noticed you have a little voice in your head that talks to you? We all experience this – it's called *self-talk* or our *inner voice*. What sort of things does it say to you? Are they positive or negative? Are they kind or critical? Without even realising it, we can often be harsh and critical to ourselves. Can you think of a time you've criticised yourself? Perhaps you made a mistake or said something you regretted to someone and chastised yourself afterwards. Or have you ever been angry with yourself when something didn't go to plan? Have you ever beaten yourself up internally for making a bad choice that you later regretted? Can you remember what your inner voice said after one of these incidents and how it made you feel? In contrast, can you also remember a time when your inner voice said something positive? For example, it told you that you'd done well at something or that you're likeable and lovable. How did that make you feel? Which experience did you prefer?

When we like ourselves, our inner voice becomes our best friend. It encourages us, builds us up and reminds us to look after ourselves. Other people's words and opinions aren't the basis for how we feel about ourselves – we are. If we like ourselves, we can more easily forgive and accept ourselves when things go wrong. And we can genuinely celebrate success when life goes well (as we believe we deserve it). If we like ourselves, it's easier to recover from setbacks. And we can also better accept the different seasons of life – with their highs and lows, good and bad outcomes.

Conversely, when we don't like ourselves, our self-talk is likely to be negative and critical. Negative self-talk loves to remind us of our past mistakes and current failings. When we make mistakes, which all of us invariably will, our inner voice becomes our arch-enemy, rubbing salt in the wound, telling us, *'I told you so.'* It will jump at any chance to 'prove' that we're a failure.

Unsurprisingly, negative thinking is linked to low mood and depression. [3] Negative self-talk can hold us back on our journey to liking ourselves as we constantly hear a critical running commentary in our heads. This can be especially true when we go through a difficult time as it's easy to blame ourselves and think negatively about ourselves when things go wrong (which they sometimes will).

REASONS TO LIKE YOURSELF MORE

Let me ask you, how could liking yourself more impact your well-being in positive ways? Would you like to experience these changes in your life? I'm hoping the answer is yes! In the next few chapters, we'll think about how to achieve these changes. We'll look at how to recognise negative thoughts and how to replace them with a kinder, more positive way of thinking. We'll also look specifically at how you can grow your self-esteem and increase your level of self-acceptance.

AS YOU LEARN TO LIKE YOURSELF MORE:

- You'll feel happier.
- You'll grow in confidence.
- You'll take greater care of yourself.
- You'll be more motivated to eat well and exercise.
- You'll be more resilient to life's knock-backs.
- You'll be more able to accept praise when things go well.
- You'll find it easier to accept your mistakes.

SOME EXERCISES TO HELP YOU LIKE YOURSELF MORE

1. RECOGNISING WHAT YOU DO AND DON'T LIKE ABOUT YOURSELF

We subconsciously weigh up and evaluate ourselves all the time. This evaluation can come from other people - for example, through comments in person and online, marks on essays, invitations to parties, messages on social media, and from our own thoughts, feelings and interpretation of events. However, often we don't spend any time considering how we *feel* about ourselves or the impact these things have on us. In this exercise, fill in Table 1 with examples of things you do and don't like about yourself. The point of this isn't to highlight all your flaws, but to help you recognise areas where you may need to work on liking yourself. If you end up with a long list of things you don't like about yourself, it doesn't mean you're a bad or unlikeable person, but that perhaps you need to focus on liking yourself more.

Table 1: Things I do and don't like about myself (both internal and external attributes)

THINGS I LIKE ABOUT MYSELF	THINGS I DON'T LIKE ABOUT MYSELF
I'm kind and thoughtful (internal)	I'm disorganised (internal)
I have nice hair (external)	I have spotty skin (external)

2. HOW DO YOU FEEL LIKED?

Having considered the importance of liking yourself, now let's spend a little time considering where your ability to feel liked comes from. Is it from inside yourself or is it from other people? Consider one of your examples from Table 1 that you like about yourself. Why do you like this about yourself?

- Is it because other people have said this is a positive attribute in you?
- Is it because you've had a positive response to this attribute on social media?
- Is it because your self-talk speaks positively about this attribute?

For example, say you've written *'I'm kind and thoughtful'*. Why do you think this? On reflection, perhaps you realise that your school reports often say this, so you've begun to believe it, or friends have commented on how kind you are. Or perhaps you've written *'I have nice glossy hair'*. You realise this is because people often comment on your hair or that the hairstyles you post receive a lot of *likes* on TikTok. None of these ways to receive affirmation are wrong (they are, in fact, very important, as we all need encouragement). However, it's equally important to be able to like these things in ourselves without needing to hear it (or see it posted) by someone else.

Now consider one of the things you don't like about yourself. Why don't you like this about yourself?

- Is it because other people have said this is a negative attribute in you?
- Is it because you've had a negative response to this attribute on social media?
- Is it because your self-talk speaks negatively about this attribute?

Think about the example *'I'm messy and disorganised'*. I wonder where this opinion has come from? Perhaps it's from your parents chastising you for leaving towels on the bathroom floor. Or is it from leaving your PE kit on the bus one too many times or forgetting your calculator and being told off? Possibly it's from much darker and deeper painful experiences, even abuse or neglect. Or in the example of *'not liking my skin'*, has this opinion come from within yourself or has that viewpoint been triggered by unkind comments online or in person? We can't undo comments and experiences, and they're bound to have an effect on us, either positively or negatively. However, recognising where other people's comments and actions have impacted us can help us build up our own inner ability to like and accept ourselves.

3. DEVELOPING SELF-LIKE

As I've mentioned, we can never fully rely on anyone else or our social media inbox to give us the affirmation, encouragement and support we need to develop a deep positive self-regard. Therefore, the best and most reliable source is actually ourselves. You alone are on tap 24/7 to be kind, caring and affirming to yourself. This might sound a little weird. But all I'm really talking about is using your self-talk to be kind and compassionate to yourself and to make choices that are good for you. Edith Eger, a Holocaust survivor who lost her family in World War Two, explains this beautifully in her book *The Gift*:

> *Remember, you're the only one you'll never lose. You can look outside yourself to feel cherished – or you can learn to cherish yourself.* [4]

Remember, no one is perfect and no one has the perfect upbringing. We all make mistakes and difficult things happen to everyone (although life isn't always fair and some people experience much more hardship than others). There are many hard challenges that you may be experiencing or have experienced. With so many difficulties around you, it may feel like it's impossible to like yourself and be happy. However, while your story is unique and can help you understand yourself, don't let your past define or dictate your future.

It is our blemishes, mistakes, experiences and imperfections that make us who we really are and give us true depth, wisdom and value. There's only one you! Remember, being self-critical won't help you find your purpose or feel happy.

A more helpful response than internal criticism is to choose a kinder and more compassionate way to look at ourselves, including accepting our flaws and forgiving ourselves. [5] Kinder ways to think include choosing to like and accept ourselves even when our behaviour doesn't meet our expectations, and choosing to be kind to ourselves even when we fail. This might seem an impossible task, but as you begin to recognise your negative self-talk and choose to respond differently, bit by bit you can change. Take the list of things you don't like about yourself in Table 1 and replace the list with a more positive view. Instead of *'I'm messy and disorganised'*, can you reframe this as *'I have the ability to be tidy and organised'*?

Remember, liking yourself is the combination of your self-esteem and self-acceptance.

The exercises at the end of Chapters 2 (on self-acceptance) and 3 (on self-esteem) will help you learn how to accept yourself more and view yourself in a positive light. This will help improve your sense of well-being, how you connect with other people, and your subsequent happiness.

CHAPTER 2

CULTIVATING SELF-ACCEPTANCE

Jemma was a highly accomplished, popular and successful 19-year-old. However, deep down she felt like a failure and that at any moment her 'less-perfect' self would be discovered. She spent hours curating the perfect image online using filters and changing the lighting and background, but the filtered images made her feel like an imposter and that she didn't really belong. She worked incredibly hard to cover up any mistakes and hated criticism. Constantly trying to be perfect online and living up to it in real life led to chronic stress and burnout.

Reluctantly, Jemma had some counselling sessions. This was incredibly hard for her as it meant sharing some of her inner fears and failures that she had worked so hard to cover up. She was even worried the counsellor would reject her and just see her faults. Eventually, she identified her need for acceptance from others and the fear that they would reject her if they knew the real Jemma. With the counsellor's help, she did some deep inner work on accepting herself, including her failures. This freed her to accept her less-than-perfect self and share her true self with others too. She also realised that her friends and family liked her just as much when she was honest and vulnerable. In fact, her relationships improved dramatically as she was more able to connect with others on a deeper level. She became more confident, happier and calmer, and lost the need to constantly prove herself.

SELF-ACCEPTANCE AND THE SELFIE

Self-acceptance is about our ability to accept ourselves as we are. It means accepting ourselves just as we are now, in this very moment, including the bits we like and the bits we don't like about ourselves. This is different to accepting ourselves *when* certain perceived imperfections improve. In the culture of perfectionism in which we live, it's often hard to recognise the importance of not being perfect. However, the reality is that none of us are perfect, however hard we try to be. We may not even notice it, but when we're saturated in social media where other people's online lives look so shiny and perfect, it can affect how we feel about ourselves. Nonetheless, striving for perfection may not actually make us happier; it's been shown that individuals with higher levels of self-acceptance and self-compassion fear failure less and have more self-confidence.[6] Remember, the successful influencer on Instagram will also have flaws and experience failures; it's just that we can't see them through their filters or the two-dimensional lens of a smartphone.

To a certain extent, all of us with an online presence portray a side of ourselves that's different to our real selves - there's a gap between our life online and our life as it really is. We often choose to only show the bits of ourselves that we like or accept (or think others will like and accept about us). This may be by simply omitting to portray the mundane or the boring and selecting the more attractive or interesting aspects of our lives instead. Our feeds may only portray our highlights, the perfect scenes and the filtered selfies. They may not show the real us behind the reel. This act of curation skews the perception others have of our lives. Although this may be subconscious, we all, to some extent, may be trying to portray a *better* self. Maybe we use online platforms to find self-acceptance through other people's approval. Or perhaps we post filtered selfies because on some level we want to 'experiment' with a new and better version of ourselves and imagine how we would feel if that were truly us.

I wonder if the degree to which we can share our real selves online is proportionate to how much we like and accept ourselves in real life? Perhaps the more we accept ourselves in real life, the more willing we are to share our authentic selves. In reality, contrary to our instinctive desire to hide our imperfections, allowing trusted people to see our real selves enables us to connect and belong. It is when we're prepared to share our vulnerabilities with others that our ability to connect with them grows. And it is a connection to others that brings meaning, purpose and belonging. Brené Brown, a professor, lecturer and author, expresses this beautifully in her book *The Atlas of the Heart*. She explains that our level of self-acceptance dictates our willingness to share our authentic selves and, therefore, our ability to connect:

Because we can feel belonging only if we have the courage to share our most authentic selves with people, our sense of belonging can never be greater than our level of self-acceptance. [7]

This ability to be authentic starts with self-acceptance; if we don't like and accept our real selves, we're unlikely to be able to share this deeper and less-perfect side with others. We can only find true freedom when we stop trying to be perfect and accept ourselves as we are, and allow others to see our real selves too. [8]

DISCONNECTION

When looking at this from the opposite angle, you may recognise a lack of self-acceptance behind some of your glossier posts on social media. In posting only your perfect self, you may be hiding the bits of you that you don't like or accept (or covering them up with a filter), inadvertently *growing* disconnection with others, as they're not seeing the real you.

Disconnection is particularly relevant in today's culture of online influencers and selfie posting. If we analyse social media posts, especially the heavily curated ones, we see that they often resonate a lack of self-acceptance. The filters, spectacular backdrops and lighting show an underlying desire to portray a *better* or *more acceptable version of themselves*. However, in reality for those living in an online sphere, it must be an incredibly lonely path to share so much online but to be known so little – to create an image online that is, in reality, impossible to live up to.

A recent online campaign highlighted the hidden face of depression. It showed happy, beaming selfies of many young people that they'd posted online. There is a horrible catch – just hours later, they each died by suicide. From the uploaded photo, you'd never have dreamt that they were contemplating taking their own lives and would in fact complete suicide. Another recent story in the media was of a teenager who'd become so addicted to posting Snapchat images of herself using filters that she didn't go outside for over a year. She hid inside because she couldn't bear the thought of people seeing her in real life, feeling she wasn't as beautiful as her curated online image. [9] These are extreme examples, but to some extent every one of us who has an online presence chooses to portray a better version of ourselves.

VALIDATION

Validation is the feeling that others approve of or accept us, or *something* that gives us that feeling. Posting on social media can seem like the easiest and quickest way to find this much-needed feeling of approval. We all know what this feels like: we post a photo and instantly receive lots of *likes* and comments, giving us the validation we *think* we need and what we *want* to hear. It gives us the message that we're loved and valued, as well as a large dose of the feel-good chemical dopamine to make us feel better. Online validation even comes with a numerical counter; we can literally see the number of people who like us! Validation in the real world is harder; it's much more complicated and less reliable than simple *likes* and comments. Real relationships are unreliable and changeable; it's difficult to know if we really belong and what other people think of us. No wonder posting on social media is so popular. We can receive instant online validation with one click of a button.

CYBERBULLYING

The problem, however, is when you base how you feel about yourself on other people's opinions of you. Especially if those opinions come via social media and from people who hardly know you (or don't know you at all). It might feel okay in the short term if the comments are positive, but it still means you're learning to judge yourself based on other people's opinions, not your own. And what if the comments aren't positive? It can be really hurtful when people make abusive or harmful comments online, something which is incredibly common. Negative comments can also come in the form of parental criticism, judgement from peers or teachers' disapproval. These can damage how you feel about yourself. The problem with such comments is that, whatever the source, it's too easy to believe them, especially if you already have a low view of yourself. They can tap into your own feelings that you're not good enough and make you feel terrible. Even a single negative comment can confirm your worst fears: that you're unattractive, unlikeable or unlovable. Unfortunately, you can easily believe a negative comment to be 'the truth', even when it's posted by someone who doesn't know you.

According to Ofcom, over half of 12- to 15-year-olds who spend time online have seen something hurtful online in the past year.[10] If you think about it, that's a lot of negative or abusive comments!

There are countless people every day posting negative and harmful material to both strangers and people they know. I wonder what it is about the internet that makes it so much easier for people to post something that they wouldn't say to someone's face? Perhaps it's that they can't see the person's reaction and therefore feel more detached. Or is it that they can hide behind an anonymous account and therefore don't fear reprisal? Perhaps the ease of posting means people don't pause and think in the same way they do in real life. Or maybe it's an outlet for the person's own pain, anger or deep dislike of themselves?

> *Zane was being bullied online. He was spending hours alone in his room with his phone, where he received torrents of abuse day and night from a group of boys at school. He was utterly miserable, refusing to go to school, and had started to self-harm. Zane confided in his mother that he felt there was no way out and he was contemplating suicide. His mother didn't know what to do or how to help so booked a GP appointment. After listening to Zane, I encouraged him to block all the negative contacts on his phone or delete the apps he was being bullied on. He found this idea really difficult, and wasn't sure if he would be able to do it, or even wanted to do it.*
>
> *Several months later, I met Zane again and he was like a different person. He had managed to block the perpetrators from his social media accounts, thus separating himself from the bullies. It had put him back in control, and after a while, realising they couldn't reach him anymore, the boys had gradually given up sending horrible messages. Zane had started going out again and made a new, much more positive group of friends.*

A study by the anti-bullying charity Ditch the Label found that one in five young people has been bullied online. Of those who've been bullied, nearly a quarter self-harm as a result. Only one in five deleted the app they'd been bullied on. [11] This seems to indicate that the majority of people who've been bullied online would rather harm themselves than be disconnected from their peer group on social media. However, as with Zane, there are ways to block the bullies and move forward. However difficult it might seem, don't be scared to block them or delete the app you're being bullied on. Also, please don't believe all the negative comments, or be at the mercy of your perpetrator. Whatever the route and however difficult it might seem, try not to let other people's critical views affect how you feel about yourself (we'll look at how to do this in Chapter 5). Their opinion shouldn't affect your self-acceptance - try to think positively about yourself and accept yourself for who you really are, no matter what other people are saying.

YOU ARE ALREADY ENOUGH

Imagine how you would feel if you could accept yourself for who you are. Imagine how you might feel in the morning if your self-talk built you up for the day rather than constantly criticising you. Imagine how you'd feel if you were less afraid of failure or being discovered for who you really are.

> Let me tell you something really important: you are already enough. You don't need to change yourself or pretend to be someone you're not. The only things you need to change are the belief that you're not good enough and the Instagram filter that hides the real you. You don't need to get higher grades, have a perfect life, have more friends or look more beautiful, as none of these things will make you truly happy. You just need to try to stop comparing yourself with others and trying to post the perfect selfie.

REASONS TO ACCEPT YOURSELF:

- You're released from perfectionism.
- You're free to be the real you.
- You're allowed to make mistakes.
- You allow others not to be perfect and also to make mistakes.
- You connect more deeply with others and you feel a greater sense of belonging.
- You allow others to see the real you – you don't need to hide.
- You're able to like yourself and feel happier.

SOME EXERCISES TO HELP INCREASE SELF-ACCEPTANCE

1. PRACTISE CONGRATULATING YOURSELF - EVEN WHEN THINGS AREN'T PERFECT

Have you noticed how much easier it is to say *well done* to other people than to congratulate yourself? Have you considered that when a friend does something well but not perfectly, you're likely to focus on the positives and congratulate them? How would you speak to yourself if it had been you? Would you say well done, or would you instantly jump to the things that didn't go so well or that you would change? I expect the latter is true. As part of an inbuilt survival mechanism, our brains are set to be critical and self-judgemental (as this promotes caution and safety). This default setting doesn't help us in the search for self-acceptance and we therefore need to retrain our brains to be less self-critical. We can do this by focusing on the positives first and talking to ourselves as we would talk to our best friend.

Spend at least five minutes a day speaking positively to yourself. This can be in your head or out loud. You could be driving in the car or in the shower. Reflect on things that have gone well or choices you've made that you're proud of that day. If you've been kind to a friend or made a healthy food choice, congratulate yourself. Think of something that you *like* about yourself. Don't focus on your slip-ups but remember the little (or big) actions or events where you've succeeded. Even though life (and you) will never be perfect, allow yourself to see the good and the positive in yourself.

We recently stayed in South Africa in a basic cabin helping at a children's programme. On the cabin wall was the quote *'Life doesn't have to be perfect to be wonderful'.* This simple quote helped reframe our mindset as a family as we adapted to different food, a communal shower and a few obligatory family arguments. We returned as a family with a new motto and gratitude for life, and it's something we're very much trying to hold on to. You could adapt this quote: *'You don't have to be perfect to be wonderful.'* If you can hold on to this truth, it will transform your opinion of yourself.

2. PRACTISE SHARING YOUR IMPERFECTIONS WITH TRUSTED FRIENDS

This may not be easy at first. However, as you learn to accept your imperfections, you'll become more able to share your mistakes. Practise Exercise 1, and hopefully you'll begin to see the positives in yourself rather than the negatives. This means you'll become less self-critical and better able to tolerate your mistakes. The aim is for your self-acceptance to grow enough for you to share your imperfections and vulnerabilities more easily.

Before starting this exercise, a word of warning: choose your friends for this carefully! Choose close friends who think well of you and whom you can trust. Take things gently at first, but start sharing more of the real you, your weaknesses and vulnerabilities. The goal is that despite your weaknesses or failings, you learn to *like* yourself and realise that others do too!

IDEAS FOR SHOWING VULNERABILITY:

- Share with a close friend a weakness, vulnerability or something that hasn't gone according to plan. For example, perhaps share an argument you've had at home or a negative feeling you've had towards yourself.
- Ask your friend, if possible, to respond with compassion and acceptance, not judgement or criticism.
- Allow yourself to like and accept yourself despite this imperfection.
- Invite your friend to share something vulnerable from their life, and respond with compassion in return.
- If you don't feel able to do this with a friend, write down the imperfection in a diary and respond to yourself in the way you'd hope a kind friend would: *'I really like and value myself despite the unkind things I said to my mother earlier.'*

3. FORGIVE YOURSELF

Forgiving ourselves for past mistakes is difficult, but it's essential for setting us free from our own negative self-criticism and judgement. Forgiving ourselves is about accepting our mistakes, choosing to love ourselves anyway and moving on with our lives. Forgiveness paves the way for self-acceptance and improves our well-being and mental health. [12] Self-blame and regret are emotions that can only hold us back. Forgiving ourselves is an act of self-love and self-care.

Practising forgiveness is difficult as there's no set formula for how to do it, and it doesn't always make sense. However hard it is, though, it's worth it, even if it takes some time. Forgiveness is a choice not a feeling, but when we make the choice, the feelings can follow. You'll know you've forgiven yourself (or someone else) when you feel lighter and more emotionally free. When you've forgiven yourself, you may also stop thinking about particular past events and focus on the present instead.

You may be unnecessarily blaming yourself for difficult life events which almost certainly won't be your fault. For example, you may blame yourself for your parents' divorce – remembering all the times you were challenging and concluding falsely that this was the reason they split up. Or you may remember unkind words you've spoken to others, or arguments you had with friends or siblings.

SIGNS THAT YOU MAY NEED TO FORGIVE YOURSELF:

- You often think back to things that have gone wrong and blame yourself.
- You spend a lot of time reflecting on past mistakes.
- You're often angry for no apparent reason.
- You suffer from unexplained low moods and sadness.
- You have conversations with yourself in your head about yourself or other people.

KEYS TO HELP YOU FORGIVE YOURSELF:

- No one is perfect; we all make mistakes and need a second chance.
- Forgiveness is a choice - we choose to set ourselves free by choosing to forgive.
- It's beautiful; forgiveness makes the world a better place.
- Forgiveness frees us from anger and resentment.

HOW TO FORGIVE YOURSELF:

Forgiveness is a process. Forgiving ourselves isn't simply letting ourselves off the hook, but is about accepting our mistakes and choosing to show ourselves compassion and kindness anyway. You can use the following steps to help you with the process: [13]

- Recognise how you're feeling and where it's due to a mistake or action for which you haven't forgiven yourself. This may involve feelings of guilt and shame.
- Accept responsibility for the mistake you've made.
- Express remorse for the mistake.
- Choose to treat yourself with kindness and compassion, despite the mistake.
- If possible, try to make amends for the mistake. Apologise to anyone else involved and to yourself for the hurt/harm you've caused.
- Try to find ways to learn from the mistake.
- Commit to behaving differently in the future.

4. CHALLENGE YOURSELF TO BE MORE AUTHENTIC ONLINE

Each of us has a part to play in changing and challenging the online culture of perfectionism. Imagine the collective impact if we all started being more authentic online. The online culture would change. We can be a *thermostat* (set the online tone) rather than a *thermometer* (react to the online tone).

Authenticity is becoming more valued. For example, there's a growing movement of online campaigns encouraging social media users to post selfies without using a filter. These campaigns aim to highlight the damage filters can do to people's mental health - with their ability to brighten our skin, change our nose shape or plump up our lips. [14]

In this exercise, we'll consider some simple, achievable steps towards sharing more of your authentic self online.

WAYS TO BE MORE AUTHENTIC ONLINE:

- **Consider changing who can see your posts** (either by unfollowing people or changing your settings to private). Think about removing people from your friends or contacts list who you don't know or who make you feel worse about yourself.
- **Consider taking the *likes* and comments off your posts** (where available on certain apps) so that you're not looking for or needing a specific response from your posts.
- **Try posting without extra makeup or filters on.** Post a photo of you as you are in this moment, your authentic self. This may feel like a difficult task. At first it might make you feel nervous and exposed. Perhaps start with just posting to one or two friends, even explaining that you're going makeup and filter free. You can gradually increase the number of people you post to until you start to find it easier. Hopefully, you'll begin to feel free and liberated, especially if the comments are off!

- **Try to present a balanced view of your life online so people can see the real you.** Consider including the mundane and the ordinary and sharing a bit of the backstory. Behind every perfect photo isn't necessarily a perfect day. Don't be afraid to share the blisters you got on the way to the viewpoint or the argument you had before your gourmet meal. These details help people relate to and know the real you. However, try not to overshare (by giving too much detail to too many people).
- **Try to post less and spend less time on social media** (as this has been shown to improve well-being!).[15] We'll look at how you can spend less time online in Chapter 11. Write down your happy experiences and take time to enjoy the real beauty of a moment. Try to live in the moment and be free to be you. Taking away the camera lens allows you to enjoy and absorb the experience and not just focus on getting the perfect picture. These are your special moments and memories; they don't need to be validated by others. The only person whose experience really counts is yours. Don't waste beautiful moments worrying about sharing them with others!

CHAPTER 3

BUILDING SELF-ESTEEM

Ben's mum was really worried about him. He was spending more and more time alone in his room. He was refusing to go to school and had started to self-harm. His parents had split up last year, and he was refusing to see his dad, who had a new partner and baby. Ben was also having a difficult time at school. He'd got into a couple of fights and he felt like no one was on his side. Ben felt alone and isolated and was struggling to cope. He blamed himself for his parents splitting up and dwelt on very negative thoughts about himself.

When Ben came to see me, his head was down and he didn't want to talk. However, bit by bit and over several appointments, Ben shared how he was feeling. Together, we established that life events over the past few years had really impacted his self-esteem. Ben began to recognise his negative self-talk and rebuild his self-confidence. He also realised that spending lots of time on his own in his room made him feel less happy. Armed with this knowledge and more support, he was able to get some mentoring at school and set himself some simple challenges to start going out again. He began mountain biking with some old friends from primary school and even cooked a family meal once a week. Bit by bit, his confidence improved and his mood lifted.

WHAT IS SELF-ESTEEM AND WHY DOES IT MATTER?

Self-esteem is something people often talk about but don't really understand. However, it's such a vital part of our personality that it's really important to understand what it is and why it has such a big impact on our well-being. Self-esteem has two parts: 1) how we see ourselves; and 2) how we evaluate our role in the events that happen to us. The first part (how we see ourselves) is a bit like looking at ourselves in an imaginary internal mirror. The internal reflection is our estimation of how successful, likeable and able we are, or how positive or negative our attitude is towards ourselves. The second part (self-evaluation) is how we interpret and internalise events which have happened to us (both good and bad). This is like a pair of imaginary glasses through which we interpret the world and judge our role in it. Both our internal mirror and the imaginary glasses can give us a real or a warped view of ourselves and how we see the world, depending on our underlying self-esteem.

> Importantly, self-esteem is simply our *current view* of ourselves and our role in the world and is therefore something we can *change* and *improve*.

(Try to remember this as you read this chapter, and there are exercises at the end of the chapter to help you do this.)

Someone with good self-esteem will have a healthy (but realistic) view of themselves, and research has shown people with good self-esteem are more likely to be happy. [16] With good self-esteem, when we look in our internal mirror, we see a true reflection. We don't have to be perfect to have good self-esteem. Having an optimistic but realistic view of ourselves doesn't mean just thinking we're brilliant at everything, but it allows us to see ourselves in a true light. Knowing and liking ourselves and having a balanced but positive view of who we are – these are essential elements of the healthy selfie. Good self-esteem doesn't just improve our day-to-day view of ourselves; it also reduces our risk of developing depression. [17] When healthy, our self-esteem can help ground us in difficult times and give us the inner strength to cope. Healthy self-esteem also creates a positive ability to change and develop as a person and is a predictor of future success and well-being. It helps keep us motivated and gives us a belief in ourselves, which helps us maintain our well-being.

On the other hand, if you have low self-esteem, you have a warped view of your true self. This warped view of yourself can impact every area of your life, as you interpret everything that happens to you through a negative bias. It's a bit like wearing a strong pair of prescription glasses which negatively skew how you see everything. The world becomes blurry. The blurry view impairs everything you see and feel about yourself. It doesn't matter how many people tell you that you're successful, likeable or good at certain things - if you're wearing the wrong glasses (a warped view of yourself), you won't be able to believe it. When you have low self-esteem, you see your strengths, successes and character attributes tinged by the untrue lens of failure; or maybe you can't even see them at all. It means you might find it harder to listen to those who compliment you because you don't feel worthy of it. Or you can't appreciate fully when things go well and you deflect the praise.

People with low self-esteem tend to have a low regard for themselves. This may play out internally with a critical inner voice and negative thoughts. On the outside, it may hold you back by lowering your confidence and create a need for everything to be perfect (as this makes you feel better about yourself). Low self-esteem also makes you vulnerable to life's stresses and failures and can lower your resilience (the ability to bounce back when things go wrong) as you believe you don't have the necessary coping mechanisms or inner strength. Remember, though, this is just your *perception* that you can't cope. It may well be that you can; the problem is that you've got a negative view of yourself!

We talked about the importance of our inner voice in the last chapter. Our inner voice is key to how we feel about ourselves. If we have negative thoughts and beliefs about ourselves, they'll feed into negative self-esteem. On the other hand, if we have a positive inner voice, this can feed into positive self-esteem (which helps us like and accept ourselves).

Pause for a moment and think about any thoughts and beliefs that you've had about yourself in the last day or so. Think about something that's gone well and an area of your life that you're proud of. How does thinking about that experience make you feel? Now consider something that you're struggling with, or a difficult experience. How do those thoughts make you feel? It's a tiny example, but I imagine that considering the positive experience made you feel temporarily happier, whilst dwelling on the negative event probably brought up some negative emotions (and may have even triggered more negative thoughts) and made you feel less good about yourself (sorry!). Imagine this micro example happening in your brain all the time. Every time you process a thought, it impacts how you feel about yourself, which affects your self-esteem and how happy you feel. Remember that it's hard to be happy if you don't like yourself.

Our *inner voice* is key to how we *feel* about ourselves.

RECOGNISING LOW SELF-ESTEEM

Table 2: Self-esteem quiz

Tick the statements that apply to you. This will help you work out whether you have low self-esteem. Calculate your score out of 25.

	TICK IF IT APPLIES TO YOU
I don't value myself.	
I often feel like a failure, even when things go well.	
I don't like myself. I post online to feel better about myself.	
I have experienced significant rejection in my life.	
I feel unattractive. I use filters and editing apps to change the bits of me I don't like.	
I compare myself to others (online and in person) and come off worse. I want to be more like the people I view online.	
I put myself down in my head, and I'm very critical of myself.	
I find it hard to stand up for myself.	
I like to be in control of everything.	
Other people don't tend to like or notice me.	
I regularly have negative thoughts about myself. I often feel low and down about myself.	
I find it difficult to believe in myself.	
I focus on the mistakes I make, not the things that go well.	

I have bouts of unexplained sadness; I cry a lot.

I find it hard to believe people like me.

I get angry or irritable easily.

There are parts of my body I really don't like.

I am reluctant to put myself forward for things, as I'm afraid I'll fail.

I find it difficult to accept compliments from people.

I avoid confrontation.

I tend to be a perfectionist.

I hate being criticised, and I take ages to recover.

I need lots of reassurance from those around me.

I sometimes get in situations where people take advantage of me. I find it hard to create boundaries.

I am a people pleaser. I do things I'd rather not do to make people like me (including things I post online).

Adapted from *Thrive.* [18]

My score .... /25. A higher score suggests that you may have lower self-esteem. A score of more than five may indicate that you have low self-esteem.

HOW SELF-ESTEEM IS FORMED

Self-esteem is formed every day by the events that happen to us and how we subconsciously interpret them. The same life event can happen to two different people and have a completely opposite effect, depending on their self-esteem and underlying personality traits. It's a two-way street - a life event can affect our self-esteem, but our self-esteem can also affect how a life event impacts us.

Imagine two young people with different levels of self-esteem failing their driving test on the same day with the same examiner. Darcie has low self-esteem, and as she already struggles to like and accept herself, this failure triggers an out-of-proportion response. She puts herself down and calls herself stupid. Her interpretation of the event further lowers her self-esteem as she blames and criticises herself for failing. On the other hand, Chase has a healthier view of himself and can recognise where he made simple mistakes that led him to fail. Chase can consider the situation with a more balanced view and healthy self-reflection. He reflects that with more practice and confidence, he'll pass next time. Chase also reminds himself that lots of people fail their driving test and that it isn't the end of the world! Despite failing his test, Chase can grow his self-esteem and resilience through the event, because he can look at it from a different perspective.

So why is it that two people can have such different views of themselves? Most children start their early years happy and carefree. Unfortunately, life events, words spoken and personal hurts can dig away at a child's sense of self. However, the real deterioration in self-esteem occurs at around 12 years of age, when self-esteem is thought to be at its lowest. The transition from childhood to adolescence can be a rocky road. Puberty, secondary school and the pressure to conform can become a melting pot of negative self-talk. It's no surprise that this can be a tough period for young people, and in today's pressure-driven society, not everyone emerges unscathed. If this sounds familiar to you, I don't need to remind you how difficult this period of life is.

When talking to a young person who's feeling unhappy, I always try to find out why they're feeling like this. Sometimes there's a 'trigger' (a really difficult life circumstance) that they're going through or have been through (for example, a family bereavement, parental divorce or sexual abuse). However, for many young people there's no definitive reason why they're feeling unhappy, but I often find that they have low self-esteem and self-acceptance that's linked to their use of social media.

SOCIAL MEDIA AND SELF-ESTEEM

In 2017, psychologist and professor Jean Twenge wrote an article that attributed the rise in mental health problems in teenagers to their smartphones. She highlighted the dramatic rise in mental health problems in American teenagers since 2011 and the parallel rise in smartphone ownership and social media use:

> *The twin rise of the smartphone and social media has caused an earthquake of a magnitude we've not seen in a very long time, if ever. There is compelling evidence that the devices we've placed in young people's hands are having profound effects on their lives – and making them seriously unhappy.* [19]

Now, obviously, social media and smartphones aren't all bad! The problem is that social media *can* prevent you from growing strong self-esteem (we've already discussed how important healthy self-esteem is to our happiness and well-being). If you spend significant time on social media, especially from a young age, you can unknowingly learn to depend too heavily on other people's opinions rather than your own. For example, you may take to heart negative comments or, worse still, be impacted by cyberbullying and hate messages. This will impact your inner voice (which may echo what you read about yourself on social media) and how you think about yourself (your self-esteem).

THE CACTUS AND THE BALLOON

To illustrate the effect of social media on self-esteem, we're going to consider the analogy of a cactus and a balloon.

A cactus is very robust and resilient (it's the only house plant I can keep alive!). A cactus can survive significant hardship, it doesn't need constant attention and it's happy with just a little sunlight on the windowsill and occasional watering. Imagine the cactus as representing someone with good self-esteem, who doesn't need constant praise and attention to believe in themselves. The roots represent a good foundation and the steadying factors of a strong support network. A cactus has deep enough roots to survive a drought, and the spikes characterise its ability to deflect (or at least not internalise) negative comments. A cactus grows slowly and steadily and is well-grounded and self-sufficient. When you have strong self-esteem, you also believe you can problem-solve when things are difficult. This is called self-belief and is your ability to think you have the inner resources to cope. However, not everyone has this inner sense of self-belief and this can result in having lower self-esteem.

If you have low self-esteem, you will find you are not as robust and resilient as the cactus. You need external validation to support your self-esteem, and this is like blowing up a balloon. When you blow up the balloon, it grows quickly, is beautiful and eye-catching, and gives you a quick dopamine fix. Like the balloon, low self-esteem inflates quickly with admiration and positive attention (for example, *likes* on social media). However, when you pop an inflated balloon, it deflates in seconds. If you have low self-esteem, this happens when you receive criticism or negativity; you can take it personally and feel negatively towards yourself. Similarly, someone with low self-esteem depends on the world's opinion of them to feel good. No one is immune to criticism, but the more dependent you are on others' views, the harder it will hit you. The person with low self-esteem also has less ability to believe they can cope. This means they might feel powerless to control their destiny or find solutions within themselves when things go wrong.

In today's social media world, it's easy to seek praise and approval from online platforms. However, this can negatively impact your view of yourself and in turn actually reduce self-esteem. The good news is that you can rebuild and restore your self-esteem.

Illustration 1: The cactus and the balloon

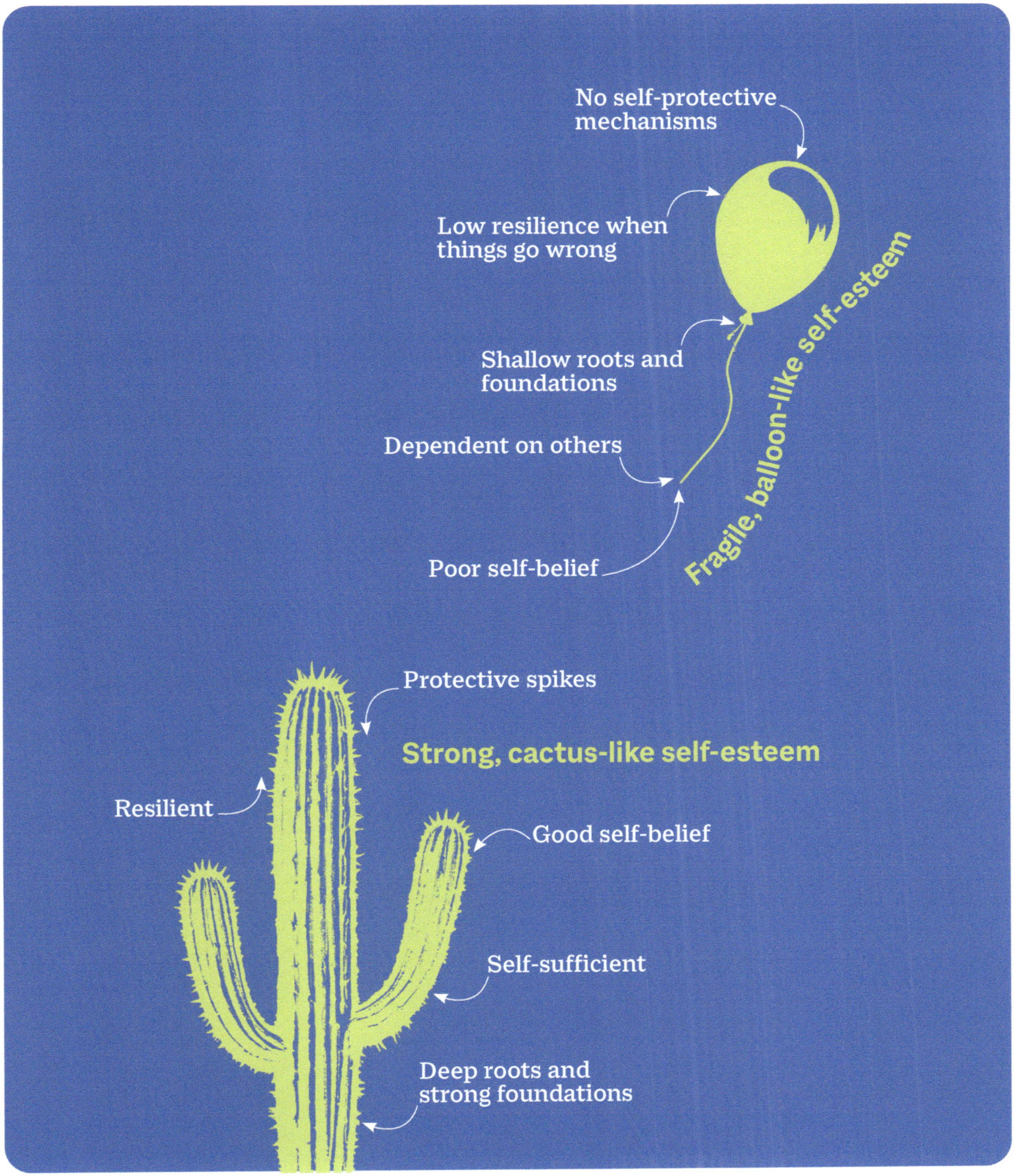

The good news is that you can rebuild and restore your self-esteem.

GROWING SELF-ESTEEM

You may have scored highly in the quiz, or some of the things you've read about low self-esteem may resonate with you. Don't panic! The key to growing your self-esteem is simply this: knowing that **self-esteem is your *current* evaluation of yourself and you can change it**. Your self-esteem isn't set in stone, and nor is it dictated by anyone else. You can improve your self-esteem – there are exercises at the end of this chapter you can use to do this.

Building your self-esteem is about learning to positively redefine how you see yourself. Armed with this knowledge, you can choose how you interpret events and train your brain to be more positive. **It's you alone who chooses the viewpoint of your story.** In your pursuit of a healthier selfie, changing the lens through which you view yourself is essential. If your filter is inherently negative, you can train yourself to put a more positive angle on events and see yourself more positively. You can set yourself free from negative self-talk and instead believe in and like yourself. **The road to freedom begins when you realise that you have the power to choose your path.**

REASONS TO BUILD YOUR SELF-ESTEEM:

- There's only one you, and you're worth it.
- It will increase your resilience to knock-backs.
- You'll be able to grow and learn when things go well.
- You'll feel happier and lighter.
- You'll have a more positive mindset.
- It will help you to have loving and mutually positive friendships and relationships.
- No one else can do it for you.
- It's better than living with the alternative of low self-esteem.

SOME EXERCISES TO BUILD YOUR SELF-ESTEEM

If you've recognised that you have low self-esteem, here are some powerful exercises to help you improve it.

1. KEEP A HAPPY LIST

This is an incredibly useful exercise for growing your self-esteem. Each day, write down a list of positive experiences and reflect on them. Start the list by thinking of ten positive things that have happened recently. You can use Table 3 for this, or you can keep a list on your phone or in a diary. You may find it difficult to think of ten things, but they will be there. Write down just one positive thing that happened if that's all you can think of to begin with. They can be really simple things (like making a cup of tea for your mum or completing your essay). The momentum and change will come as you keep this up every day. Gradually, your list will grow. Try to look at the list at least three times a day so that you keep reflecting on the positive things in your life. Spend time every day going over your list and add to it if you can. It's lovely to remember that special hug or the card someone wrote you that you might have otherwise forgotten. Doing this helps your mind to process and remember the good things in your life, rather than allowing the brain to go to its default negative setting. The more you reflect on positive experiences, the more you will benefit. [20]

As part of the exercise, also write down what it was about the experience that made it positive and what you'd say to your best friend if they had the same experience. One of the most powerful ways to improve our self-talk (and subsequently self-esteem) is to look at the experience from a best friend's perspective. Most of us are very good at encouraging and being positive with a friend but find it so much harder to talk to ourselves in that way. So reflect on what you'd say if your best friend had your experience, then tell yourself that same thing. For example, when Ben started mountain biking again, he told me, *'It was alright. Anyone could do it.'* I then asked him to imagine his best friend had been feeling down and had taken up a hobby again, and what would he say to him? Instead, he said, *'Wow, that's awesome! It must have taken so much guts – you nailed it!'* Ben could start to see his experience from a more positive perspective when he looked at it from his best friend's perspective. It enabled him to change his self-talk from a constant mantra of negativity to one that was more uplifting and positive.

Finally, also reflect on what you've learnt from the experience. This will help to reinforce the positive learning and help to maintain change (which is always difficult). By reflecting on his happy list, Ben learnt that he was happier when he was doing something that he enjoyed. This helped motivate him to get out of his bedroom and see his friends or play sport. He was able to set himself weekly goals and timetabled activities, so he wasn't so bored or alone.

Table 3: The happy list

POSITIVE SITUATION	WHAT MADE THIS EXPERIENCE POSITIVE
I met a friend today even though I was feeling down.	It was nice to get out.
I completed my English essay.	It felt great handing it in on time and being able to enjoy a guilt-free weekend.

Adapted from *Thrive*.[21]

WHAT I'D SAY TO MY BEST FRIEND IF THEY EXPERIENCED THIS EVENT

Well done for going to meet your friend, even though it would have been easier to cancel.

You're amazing! Great work!

WHAT I'VE LEARNT FROM THIS

I feel better when I spend time with friends.

It's better to get my homework done, even if it's not perfect.

2. LOOK AFTER YOURSELF

Part of growing your self-esteem is looking after yourself and being kind to yourself. That doesn't mean being selfish; instead, you acknowledge your needs and make choices that allow you to look after yourself. Think of something special you can do for yourself and take the time to do it. This can be something you enjoy doing, like going to the cinema or seeing a friend, or something that makes you feel good, like exercise or enjoying some downtime.

Remember that although you may enjoy time on social media, it may not be making you feel good about yourself. What are the things that make you happy? Consider the activities and pastimes that lift your mood. Try to spend more time doing these things - reschedule your diary to make space for them in your week! Your mood will lift as you prioritise doing something you like and enjoy. Balance the things you don't like (essays, work, chores, school) with things you do like. Reward yourself for completing a task you don't like with something that you do.

We all know that being kind to others is important, but it's equally vital to be kind to yourself. Remember, self-care isn't selfish; it's essential for your well-being.

IDEAS FOR HOW TO BE KIND TO YOURSELF:

- Instead of stressing over a to-do list, keep a 'done' list and celebrate your accomplishments.
- Make time for the things you enjoy without feeling guilty.
- Take at least ten minutes every day to do something that brings you joy, such as taking a relaxing bath, going for a walk, reading a book, calling a friend or listening to music.
- Treat yourself to a massage, pedicure or haircut.
- Make exercise a regular part of your routine and prioritise it in your schedule.

- Try to avoid unhealthy snacks and aim to eat plenty of fruits and vegetables.
- Only seek out online content that uplifts you and makes you feel good about yourself, whether it's inspiring quotes, uplifting stories or hilarious memes.

3. BE KIND TO OTHERS

One of the best ways to grow self-esteem is to be kind to others. It gives us a sense of purpose and improves our well-being. In a low moment, try being kind to someone. It's incredible how being kind can reset our mood and mindset - being kind shifts the brain's gear by releasing oxytocin (a happy hormone). This promotes feelings of gratitude and well-being.

Being kind also makes the world a better place for those receiving the kindness. My daughter was recently in hospital, and the staff's small (but very significant) acts of kindness amazed us. We'll never forget the healthcare assistant who made her a homemade chocolate milkshake when she couldn't eat, or the porter who brought her tissues when she was crying in pain. It may have just felt like part of their job for these individuals, but their acts of kindness kept us going during a traumatic period.

Kindness can help distract you from negative thoughts and feelings and help you feel more satisfied with your life as you focus on helping others.

Frequently at suppertime, I ask my children two questions:

- What's the kindest thing you've done today?
- What's the kindest thing someone has done for you?

These two questions are incredibly powerful. They help you reflect and process where you've been kind, and thinking about who's been kind to you allows you to appreciate others' acts of kindness and recognise that people care about and look after you.

IDEAS FOR HOW TO BE KIND:

- Start a conversation with someone who appears to be lonely or left out at school or college.
- Buy a drink for a friend, or make your parent or carer a cup of tea.
- Text or tell someone something you like about them.
- Invite people to your home (if you live at home remember to ask your parents or carers first).
- Thank someone for something they've done for you.
- Phone or message a friend who's having a difficult time.
- Smile more at people.
- Ask a friend to go for a walk or to hang out together.
- Give money to a good cause that you care about (it doesn't matter how small the amount is).
- Get into the habit of telling a friend or family member if they've done something well.
- Remember elderly friends and relatives and get in touch with them.
- Bake cakes or take round little gifts for your neighbours.

4. PRACTISE GRATITUDE

Practising being thankful is another powerful tool for improving self-esteem. It's the antidote to negativity and low mood - practising gratitude has been shown in studies to reduce symptoms of anxiety and depression. [23] Gratitude helps us to get things in perspective and to remember that there's always something positive, however small it might be. Practising gratitude creates an upward spiral of positivity. As you're thankful and thank others, it also improves *their* well-being and encourages them to do the same. It's harder to remain in a negative mindset when we focus on being thankful. It might feel counter-intuitive, or like the last thing you feel like doing, but I encourage you to do it anyway as you will feel better.

KEEP A GRATITUDE JOURNAL

Every day in your journal, reflect on aspects of your life that you're thankful for. Use these prompts to help you.

- My favourite moment of the day......
- A person I'm thankful to have in my life......
- Something beautiful that put a smile on my face......
- Some positive news......
- Something I've achieved that I'm proud of......

PRACTISE THANKING PEOPLE

Practise thanking people - for example, the person at the checkout, or a teacher for helping you with your essay. You can thank people in person or get into the habit of sending messages thanking people for things they've done for you. Enjoy how it makes you feel. Small acts can make such a difference to someone else. Think how good it makes *you* feel when someone thanks and acknowledges you for something. When patients tell me the difference I've made to them, it gives me the strength and encouragement I need to help the next person. You have the power to help other people experience the same thing and build their (and your) self-esteem simultaneously. You can create a culture of gratitude in your home, school and community.

CHAPTER 4

STOP COMPARING YOURSELF TO OTHERS

Seventeen-year-old Tia had dropped out of hairdressing college after one term. It was hard for her to make friends and she didn't enjoy the course. She was now living at home with her mum, stepdad and three-year-old half-brother. She said she felt too low and anxious to look for a job and spent most of her time in her room. Tia had lost touch with friends from school and college. Even if she'd wanted to go out, she was socially isolated and felt she had no one to meet up with.

Tia came to me for help with her mood. During the consultation, it transpired that Tia spent endless hours a day alone in her room on social media. Whilst at college, she'd viewed photos of her friends on nights out together. Tia had felt left out and alone as she hadn't been invited; this made her feel depressed. Although she connected with her friends on social media, seeing their lives online made her feel worse about her life. She looked at their seemingly perfect lives and compared them to her own, and that made her feel like a failure.

After meeting Tia several times, I was able to establish that the root of her unhappiness was her rock-bottom self-esteem and that she felt inadequate when she compared herself to others online. This made it hard for her to do anything, as she felt so down about herself and that she wasn't as good or pretty as her peers. We worked on building Tia's self-esteem (using some of the techniques in Chapter 3), and she received some counselling from a local charity. Eventually, Tia teased herself apart from her phone. Instead of comparing herself to others on her Instagram feed, she started spending some time volunteering in a local charity shop, which gave her a sense of purpose. She found a way out of her bedroom and into the workplace.

COMPARISON CULTURE

Whether or not we recognise it, we all compare ourselves to other people! To bring meaning and purpose to our own lives, our brains are constantly weighing up and comparing us to others. Unfortunately, however, because our brains latch on to our negative attributes rather than the positive ones, we tend to fall short. And so rather than having a positive effect, comparison instead lowers our self-esteem. The author and illustrator Charlie Mackesy sums comparison up in two short sentences:

> *'What do you think is the biggest waste of time?'*
> *'Comparing yourself to others.'*[24]

Comparison is the nemesis of liking and accepting yourself, as it erodes self-esteem and self-acceptance. To like yourself more, you need to compare yourself to other people less. Comparing yourself to others can undo all the positive work you've been doing on building your self-esteem. When you compare yourself to other people, you'll always manage to find an area in which you fall short. Mo Gawdat, an author and speaker on happiness, writes in his book *Solve for Happy*:

> *It's not hard to see that we're each dealt a different hand by life. Some are taller, richer and poorer, healthier, funnier, prettier. That's why if you focus on any specific part of your life, there will always be someone who has 'more' than you. We forget the flip side of this distribution curve; each of them has 'less' than you in at least one thing.*[25]

Comparison is also the result of the success-driven society we live in, where achievement is valued over simply being. I suspect you feel under tremendous pressure to be successful, by achieving excellent grades, as well as being good at drama, sport and art! All your spare time can be filled with extracurricular activities that somehow tick an unwritten success list for parents and teachers.[26] It's an enormous pressure to bear and an unfair one; somehow society focuses on *achievements* rather than character attributes needed to be successful in life (which are eventually far more important). One of my patients told me she was so busy as an adolescent doing extracurricular activities that her mum had to practically spoon-feed her porridge whilst she got dressed for five a.m. swimming, which was followed by a long day at school, sandwiches in the car on the way to two or three extracurricular evening activities and then being helped into bed at night as she was so tired. By the time she reached university, she was exhausted and suffering from burnout and stress.

WHY DO WE COMPARE OURSELVES?

Comparison is a negative by-product of low self-esteem and low self-acceptance; it can be rooted in a need to prove your worth to yourself and to others. Or it can be an unhelpful *coping mechanism* to bolster you if you're feeling low about yourself (think back to Chapter 1 on liking yourself). And there's no doubt it's a negative consequence of a social media-driven age where other people's perfectly filtered lives are so deceptively on display for you to see. Friends and peers around you may seem to achieve so much, and as a result it's hard not to feel that you fall short. You can subconsciously turn to comparison to try to make yourself feel better. However, the very act of comparison can leave you feeling more inadequate and dissatisfied.

COMPARISON AND SOCIAL MEDIA

Adolescence is marked by a tribal mentality and a need to fit in. However, if you compare yourself to others it can, in fact, increase how much you worry that others are judging you and can leave you feeling less in control.[27] Also, it appears to be the comparison with those you don't know in person that's particularly harmful. For example, researchers have that shown frequent social media users believe that other users are happier and more successful than they are, especially when they don't know the user well offline.[28] This could be because you have no real-life comparison to compare the truth of these posts with, and you're therefore more likely to believe them.

So instead of building you up, a quick scroll on Insta can, in fact, leave you feeling *less* beautiful, *less* popular and *less* worthy than your peers. What you see during this scroll is other people's highlight reel, their filtered images and made-up backdrops. But what your brain sees is that your life comes up short - that you're *less* viewed, *less* liked or followed, and *less* acceptable than those you follow. Instead of prompting you to stop scrolling, this feeling of inadequacy may cause you to continue, as you subconsciously search for something to make you feel better. However, the longer you spend scrolling, the greater the feelings of inadequacy and dissatisfaction, which can subtly grow. If you feel lesser than your peers, you may become under-confident, worry more about what people think of you or worry more about fitting in.

OVERCOMING COMPARISON

It's essential to set our own values and achievements with our own benchmark, not other people's. Before my eldest daughter takes a test, I always ask her what she's hoping to score and encourage her to put in sufficient effort to achieve this. Rather than focusing on other people's scores, we focus on whether she's achieved the test score that she was aiming for. I'm trying to help her judge her effort as her benchmark, not other people's success. **It doesn't matter if you haven't done as well as others. What matters is whether you've achieved what you were hoping for. If not, what can you do differently next time?** This viewpoint doesn't just apply to test scores; it can be a benchmark for how we view our lives. Look at your life from the vantage point of what you like and value, and focus on these goals, not other people's goals and achievements.

As your self-esteem and self-acceptance grow, you'll find that the need to compare yourself with others reduces and that other people's lives don't matter as much. Your benchmark becomes something you set for yourself, not someone else's. Ideally, the only person you should compare yourself with is yourself! Try shifting your focus towards becoming a better person, rather than comparing yourself to others.

Are you happy with yourself? This is the only question that should matter. Are you happy with how you're looking after yourself? Does what you're thinking about make you happy? Are you happy with how you treat those around you? What are your values and are you pursuing them? Ultimately, what kind of person do you want to become, and are you on track to be that person?

REASONS TO STOP COMPARING YOURSELF TO OTHERS:

- It's pointless and a waste of time.
- It will make you feel worse about yourself.
- It erodes your self-esteem.
- It disempowers you and your value system.
- It can make you dissatisfied and ungrateful for your life.
- It makes you focus on external signs of success rather than internal ones such as kindness or thoughtfulness. Success is about who you are as a person.

TOOLS TO HELP YOU STOP COMPARING YOURSELF TO OTHERS

1. FOCUS ON YOUR STRENGTHS AND POSITIVES

Focus on the positives in your life and what you like about yourself. Focus on what you have, not what you don't have, and what you like, not what you don't like. Make a list of things that you like about yourself and positive things in your life. It can be a mixture of specific things you like about yourself such as *'I like the fact that I have nice eyes'* and more generalised positives like *'I have a supportive family'*. Use the list to remind yourself of your strengths and to increase gratitude for your life.

2. DECLUTTER YOUR SOCIAL MEDIA

Go through your social media contacts and unfollow anyone whose posts make you feel unhappy or bad about yourself. Use the Marie Kondo (the famous Japanese tidier) technique to declutter your friends list. Go through each contact (as she encourages you to do with your belongings) and ask if they bring you joy. [29] If not, unfollow them!

3. KNOW YOUR FRIENDS

Try only being friends online with people you know in person; that way, you have a better context to understand their posts. Or only follow people who encourage you to be your authentic self and who make you feel good about yourself. For example, following people who are body positive can actually help improve your body image. [30]

4. CELEBRATE THE SUCCESSES OF OTHER PEOPLE

Celebrating others' successes can help you to succeed too! Make a point of congratulating them and consider even buying a card or gift when they do well. Remind yourself that their success doesn't make you a failure; don't compare yourself, but be inspired. Try to learn from their achievements and apply the lessons of their experiences to your life.

Celebrating others' successes can help you to succeed too!

CHAPTER 5

YOU ARE WHAT YOU THINK

Ada had been through a very traumatic life event and knew that occasionally really awful, rare events do happen. However, the reality is that the chance of dying from the flu is incredibly low. I was able to help Ada recognise her untrue thought 'If I go to university I'll die like my brother' and reframe it in a different light: 'The loss of my brother was truly awful, but that doesn't mean it will happen to me. I'm fit and well, and I'm safe and loved.' Helping Ada wasn't about ignoring her experience; recognising her trauma was incredibly important to her healing. However, she needed help recognising how her deeply traumatic past had framed her thinking in a very negative light. Once Ada realised this, she was better able to challenge her thinking and focus on the truth. Ada did go to university and is doing remarkably well.

WHAT WE THINK ABOUT AFFECTS OUR BRAINS

Like a fishing boat that casts a vast net out to sea, our minds *catch* millions of thoughts every day. However, not all of these thoughts are helpful or valuable. In a similar way that plastic waste and inedible sea-life are caught in a fishing net, negative thoughts can pollute your mind and affect your self-esteem. This is because the content of your thoughts influences how positively or negatively you feel about yourself. In the same way that a fisherman separates the valuable fish from the debris, you need to focus on useful thoughts and pay less attention to unhelpful ones. To do this you need to learn how to recognise and choose helpful and positive thoughts. Remember, what you think about affects how you feel about yourself. Focusing on positive thoughts will improve your mindset and help you feel happier.

There are an incredible 86 billion specialist nerve cells in our brains called neurons. They fire electrical and chemical impulses that enable the brain to communicate with the rest of the body. These neurons are linked with 10,000 other nerve cells to make massive information-sharing pathways. [31] We can think of these pathways as road networks of different sizes that carry information at great speed. Our brains have an incredible ability to change and adapt; every thought or action we have makes or strengthens a brain connection. The more frequently we have a particular thought, the broader and smoother the neuronal pathway will become. When a neuronal pathway is smoother and more regularly used, it becomes easier for the brain to choose that specific route. Over time our frequent thoughts become the motorways of our brains. In contrast, things we think about less frequently are like the minor roads. It's more effort for our brains to choose these pathways as they're smaller, narrower and less frequently used.

This is how our memory works. My times tables have become a very distant memory and are hard to recall, but my daughter, who's practising them regularly in school, can fire them off in seconds. My times-table neural pathways have become very small and slow, whilst hers are large and fast. Similarly, if we have repetitive negative thoughts, these pathways grow larger and become the dominant neuronal pathways of our brains. For example, say you're constantly thinking *'I'm not liked'* or *'I'm on the edge of my friendship group – no one really wants me'*. These pathways will become the path of least resistance, resulting in you more easily and frequently dwelling on these negative thoughts.

It's important to think about these pathways from the viewpoint of social media. Think about how much time you spend online every day and the content you absorb. How you spend your time online and what you see will impact your brain. If you're spending hours every day looking at other people's apparently perfect lives and (subconsciously or even consciously) feeling less positive about yourself, this will become the pathway of least resistance in your brain. Or, if you're being bullied online or viewing harmful content, consider how much more the brain will become hardwired to view yourself in a negative light. Anxiety can be caused by the same process, where you repeatedly dwell on a worrying thought. An extreme example of this is an anxiety disorder, where the brain gets stuck on the same worrying or anxious thoughts. It's almost like an electrical short-circuit with thoughts going round and round, caught in a never-ending loop. They're challenging to overcome because the brain keeps short-circuiting back to them again and again.

RETRAINING THE BRAIN

The good news is that because of its inbuilt capacity for change, we can retrain our brains. Our neuronal pathways can be rewired, and subsequently the positive thoughts and corresponding pathways will become our brain's main thoroughfares. As you grow these pathways it will then become easier to dwell on positive and overcoming thoughts, instead of negative ones, in the future.

> Retraining your brain is like training for a sports event - it takes daily practice and perseverance.

The exercises at the end of the chapter may be sufficient to get you started. Or you may need to engage in a course of Cognitive Behavioural Therapy (CBT), either online or in person. This is a talking therapy that helps you understand how your thoughts are connected to how you feel and behave. It's been shown to reduce anxiety and low mood in adolescents. [32] CBT is available via the NHS, online courses or a private accredited therapist. [33]

HOW TO CHANGE THE WAY YOU THINK

ARE YOUR THOUGHTS TRUE, KIND AND HELPFUL?

Litmus paper is used in chemistry to test if a substance is an acid or alkali. It turns blue in an alkali liquid and pink in acid. Amazingly, in nature the hydrangea plant does a similar thing, but the colours are reversed. If you plant them in alkaline soil, they grow pink flowers; conversely, they grow blue flowers in acidic soil. Now, take a moment to think about your recent thoughts. **Are they true, kind and helpful?** I use this simple three-part test to help young people consider their thoughts and recognise where their thinking is holding them back. It's a litmus-paper test for your thoughts!

By applying this three-part test to your thoughts (are they true, kind and helpful?), you can begin to recognise and challenge harmful thinking. This helps you understand if a thought or thought pattern is helpful to you and contributing to your well-being (or doing the opposite). It's often not apparent which thoughts are harmful to you until you *think* about your *thinking*. You may not recognise that certain thoughts are untrue, unkind or unhelpful, but instead mistake them for reality.

It's important to be mindful of what you consume on social media, as it can impact how you view yourself. From fake news to hurtful comments, it's easy to unknowingly adopt others' opinions about you. This means you can subtly believe lies about you based on the opinions of others (often people you don't even know). For example, you may receive inappropriate 'jokey' comments on a TikTok video about your weight. Although you may or may not *believe* these comments, they may subtly influence how you feel about yourself. Online gaming can also be an incredibly competitive and harsh field where players are very critical of others' mistakes. It's become *normal* to receive abusive comments, and possibly say abusive comments back, which affects how players think about themselves.

ARE YOUR THOUGHTS TRUE?

MANY NEGATIVE THOUGHTS WE HAVE ARE SIMPLY NOT TRUE

We can easily make the mistake of believing every thought we have is true, whereas our thoughts are, in fact, merely our *interpretations* of events. When we dwell on a thought, we can perceive it as reality. In fact, though, it's just our opinion or our interpretation of an event and we don't always get it right!

The first key step is to realise that just because you're having a thought, that doesn't mean it's actually reality. For example, you may wrongly interpret a friend not replying to your message to mean that they don't like you anymore, when in fact their phone had run out of battery and they hadn't seen your message. Or you may have a severe headache for several days and wrongly start worrying that you have brain cancer or meningitis, but in reality you pulled a neck muscle leaning over your laptop and this has triggered a headache (this is a very common cause of headaches). You might start thinking that a low number of *likes* on the selfie you posted on Instagram means that people don't like you or that they think you're unattractive; however, in reality people didn't see the post thanks to the algorithms sending your post to the bottom of their feed.

So often, especially if you have low self-esteem, you can interpret life events in a negative light. The events probably didn't even happen in the way you remember them. Your brain is often missing essential bits of information, like the real reason your friend didn't message back or why your post was ignored. We learnt earlier how by default our brains can see things in a negative light. And the more we see things in a negative light, the more these neuronal pathways will develop, forming a habit. In other words, we interpret things in a negative light because we've done it so many times before. In an attempt to make sense of the world, our brains fill in the gaps with assumptions and best guesses. Unfortunately, it rarely does a perfect job. We can fail to realise that what we're remembering, or how we interpret an event, isn't actually reality.

For example, suppose five different people witness the same event, a woman being mugged in the park. They'll all remember different bits of information and might remember the key facts differently, even though each individual is confident that their interpretation was what really happened. The witnesses will almost certainly be unaware of where they have misremembered or misinterpreted events. Their memory has become their reality.

Just because you have a thought, that doesn't mean it's true.

Just because you have a thought, that doesn't mean it's true.

In depression, because of the lack of serotonin (our happy hormone) the brain will see and interpret things in a more negative light. These negative interpretations create a vicious downward spiral that's hard to get out of. Depressive thoughts make it harder to go out and do things that make you happy, keeping you isolated and alone. For example, if you interpret your friend's lack of a reply incorrectly (that they don't like you), you'll be less likely to make contact again and meet up. I recently consulted with a 50-year-old woman with an adult-onset eating disorder. She was dangerously underweight and her small-sized clothes were falling off her. However, she was convinced she had fat thighs. Despite being dangerously thin, her belief that she was fat was her (interpretation of) reality. We'll look at how not to misinterpret thoughts a little later in this chapter.

SOME OF THE WAYS NEGATIVE THOUGHTS CAN CREEP IN:

- **Through other people's words and criticisms.** You then interpret them as reality or truth. For example, if other people constantly tell you you're not good at something or if you receive abuse online, you might believe them.
- **Through fear-based thoughts.** These thoughts are often inaccurate and based on improbable events happening in the future. You think about something awful happening and then believe this will become a reality. For example, you might worry that your dad (who's fit and well) will have a heart attack because you watched a TV programme where a character (who resembled your dad) died suddenly. Remember, no one knows what will happen tomorrow. You can't predict adverse life events.
- **Your negative interpretation of events.** It can be hard to notice when you misinterpret events as the misinterpretation is often based on a half-truth or information filtered with a negative skew by your brain. This can happen when you misinterpret an event. For example, if a friend pulls out of an arranged meet-up, you could interpret it to mean they don't like you, whilst the reality is that they'd forgotten about a family commitment.

BEING OPEN ABOUT YOUR WORRIES

It's essential to develop openness and honesty with your struggles, especially those in your head. The first step to help you not misinterpret your thoughts is to discover if they're true or not. One way to do this is by talking about your worries. When we talk about our worries, we can realise that our worst fears and anxieties are unrealistic and often very unlikely to happen. Once we realise that much of what we're worrying about isn't true, the world becomes a better place.

This is often true with health worries. You can spend days or weeks interpreting your symptoms as catastrophic and dwelling on your imminent illness or death. However, as with the headache, it's more than likely something that's not serious, like a neck spasm, a migraine or a tension headache. When you worry about your health, the outcome you fear is often based on an incorrect presumption. Hopefully, after a discussion with a doctor or wise friend (rather than *Dr Google*, which unhelpfully links common symptoms to rare diseases), you can give these fears a rational, logical explanation rather than an irrational, fear-based interpretation.

Unfortunately, life can be very challenging and sometimes the things we worry about can happen. It's not realistic to think you'll never worry. However, remember that you only need to think about the things that are *actually* happening; you don't need to go down a rabbit warren of what-ifs. The vast majority of what you're worrying about won't happen. If you just focus on the things that *are* true, you'll have the resilience and coping strategies when trouble does come your way.

You may be having a really challenging time, feel overwhelmed and be struggling to see a way through. My advice is to write down all the things you're worrying about and then divide them into worries that are true and untrue. You can then focus on the worries that are real and try to focus on looking for solutions or ways to cope with these.

> You can also dramatically improve your well-being by spending more time dwelling on positive and empowering thoughts

(we'll explore how to implement this in the exercises later in the chapter).

HOW TO REINTERPRET UNTRUE THOUGHTS

1. RECOGNISE UNTRUE THOUGHTS

The first vital step is learning to recognise negative thoughts; for example: *'My friend didn't respond to my message; therefore she must hate me'*. If you're dwelling on a worrying thought, start by writing the thought down. Rather than just presuming the thought is true, try to think about the thought objectively and analyse it.

WAYS TO CHECK IF A THOUGHT IS TRUE OR NOT:

You can use the following questions to help evaluate if a thought you're having is true or not (you can jot down your responses or use Table 4). Follow these steps for each thought:

1. Look at the facts. How likely is it to happen?
2. Ask a friend for their opinion – listen to them! Please don't ignore what they say. They probably have a better and more accurate perspective than you, as they can look at the situation objectively.
3. Look for alternative explanations that are more common or likely.
4. Decide whether the thought is true.

Table 4: Are my thoughts true?

NEGATIVE THOUGHT	WHAT ARE THE FACTS?	WHAT DOES A TRUSTED FRIEND OR FAMILY MEMBER SAY?	IS THERE AN ALTERNATIVE EXPLANATION?	IS IT TRUE?
My friend didn't message back; she must hate me.	You have been friends for years.	Why don't you message them again or call, as it's out of character?	Maybe she didn't see the message, or her phone was off.	NO!

2. REPLACE UNTRUE THOUGHTS

Once you've recognised a thought as untrue or inaccurate, you need to try to replace it with something true or positive. Every time that thought pops unwittingly into your consciousness, take the time and effort to replace it with something true. It can take hundreds of attempts to replace a thought before you realise it's stopped coming. You'll eventually disconnect the negative neuronal pathway with each successful attempt and create a new positive pathway for your thoughts to dwell on.

In Table 5, write down some of the untrue thoughts you've recognised (either from the last exercise or new ones). Now spend some time writing alternative replacement thoughts in the second column of the table.

Table 5: Replacing untrue thoughts

MY UNTRUE THOUGHT	REPLACEMENT TRUE THOUGHT Replace negative thoughts with specific opposite truths and concentrate on these instead.
My friend didn't message back; she must hate me.	We've been friends for years. There must be an alternative explanation.

You can also keep a 'positive thought replacement bank' to use when you're having negative thoughts. To do this, write a list of positive thoughts on sticky notes. When you have a negative thought, take one of your positive notes and focus on this instead.

Your success doesn't dictate your value. Your most significant achievement may simply be learning to like and accept yourself.

ARE YOUR THOUGHTS KIND? WHAT DOES YOUR INNER VOICE SAY?

Chloe was a third-year university student who struggled with perfectionism. She was studying philosophy and couldn't complete her essays. She wrote and rewrote them for days, requested extensions and still failed to submit them on time. When we explored this issue together, she realised she feared achieving anything below a 'first'. She would rather not submit than suffer the perceived failure of anything less than the perfect grade. She was sabotaging her degree in her desire for the perfect score. When she got less than 100 per cent, her inner voice went into overdrive, telling her she was useless and a failure.

THE UNKIND VOICE IN YOUR HEAD

As we've discussed, everyone has an inner voice and many people have unkind thoughts about themselves, like *'I'm useless at school'*, *'Nobody likes me'* or *'I'm unattractive'*. Unfortunately, it's easier to accept the negative, condemning voice in your head than the positive one (which, in my experience, often speaks more quietly). Perhaps you tolerate unkind, negative thoughts about yourself because you believe it's self-indulgent to listen to your positive voice. Sometimes you might believe your unkind thoughts are true, without even realising that many of them are self-critical. Or you could have unkind thoughts because you set such high standards for yourself and they're impossible to meet. This can perpetuate a cycle of *feeling* like a failure, even when the evidence is to the contrary.

> Failure can be a trigger for self-rejection and unkind self-talk. You may wrongly believe you're more lovable when you succeed. You can learn this subconsciously through your experiences in school or from overcritical parents, friends and teachers.

Our current education system rewards success and can invisibly trap you in a cycle of needing to achieve. **Remember: your success does not dictate your value. Your most significant achievement may simply be learning to like and accept yourself.** We'll look at ways to challenge your unkind voice later in this chapter.

DEVELOPING A KINDER INNER VOICE

Being kind to yourself starts with how you think about yourself. Changing how you think about yourself can change how you feel and behave. As you're kinder and more loving to yourself, you'll also become kinder in how you choose to live and the choices you make. *Kinder thoughts* lead to *kinder feelings* about yourself and *kinder behaviour* towards yourself. This means thinking about your needs and desires and balancing them with the demands of your life.

> Meeting your own needs doesn't mean being self-centred; in fact, it can help you have greater capacity for helping others.

When your behaviour changes (this may be better self-care, boundaries and friendships), this creates an upward spiral of health and well-being. Edith Eger, the author and Holocaust survivor, writes, *'It's good to be self-ish: to practice self-love and self-care.* [34] Self-compassion and self-care are vital skills in improving your well-being. [35]

HOW TO CHALLENGE UNKIND THOUGHTS

1. RECOGNISING UNKIND THOUGHTS

Have you had any unkind thoughts about yourself recently? How did they make you feel? Unfortunately, dwelling on unkind thoughts can make you feel rubbish! The good news is, you don't need to believe everything your inner voice says. Challenging unkind thoughts involves recognising them and then finding ways to change them. The aim is to retrain your inner voice to be kinder, which will make you feel happier. This is a challenging task, but remember, the brain is being rewired every time you challenge an unkind thought. Consider it like training for a marathon; changing your thoughts takes commitment and daily practice. However, bit by bit, you can build up your brain's ability to dwell on positive thoughts, and next time you'll find it easier to replace a negative thought.

To discover what you think about yourself, spend an hour or so analysing your inner voice and jot down what it's saying. You can use Table 6 or write notes on a piece of paper. Then decide if your thoughts are positive and kind or negative and unkind.

Table 6: What my inner voice is saying

SUMMARY OF MY INNER VOICE	IS IT KIND? YES/NO
I'm a really good friend	Yes

2. REPLACING UNKIND THOUGHTS

The aim of this exercise is to retrain your inner voice to be kinder and make you happier. As mentioned, your inner voice can be your worst enemy or your best friend – only you can choose. However, if you train your inner voice to be your best friend, you'll feel happier! So we're going to look at how to make your inner voice kinder.

You've already done the first step, recognising and writing down unkind thoughts. The next step is to *challenge* these thoughts. Here's how:

1. In Table 7, write down some examples of unkind thoughts.
2. Reflect on how these thoughts make you feel about yourself.
3. Write kind and positive thoughts to challenge the unkind thoughts.
4. Reflect on how the kind thoughts make you feel.

Table 7: How kind are my thoughts?

MY THOUGHT	HOW DID THAT THOUGHT MAKE ME FEEL?	ALTERNATIVE KIND THOUGHT e.g. what I'd say to my best friend	HOW DOES THE KIND THOUGHT MAKE ME FEEL?
I'm a failure as I only got a B in my essay. I'm stupid.	Worthless Like a failure	I'm imaginative and creative. I'm good at English. My grades don't define me!	I feel more positive and happier.

As you recognise that kinder thoughts improve your well-being, try to gradually increase how kind your thoughts are. Again, speak to yourself as you would your best friend. Imagine how you would feel if you only listened to your kinder inner voice.

TIPS FOR BEING KIND TO YOURSELF:

- Only speak to yourself as you would your best friend.
- Treat yourself and give yourself time to look after yourself.
- Be kind to yourself online. Pre-empt negative comments by taking back control of your feeds. Turn the comments and *likes* off on your social media accounts. You'll then be safe from negative comments or the need for other people's responses to make you feel better.
- De-friend, unfollow or block anyone who makes unkind comments about you or others.
- Each day, carry out random acts of kindness towards yourself and others.

ARE YOUR THOUGHTS HELPFUL?

WHAT IS A HELPFUL THOUGHT?

As humans we love to analyse, plan and worry, especially about the future. However, this isn't always helpful for our emotional well-being. Every day we have millions of thoughts; some are helpful and positive, whilst others are negative and unhelpful. We're now going to consider which thoughts are actually *beneficial* for our well-being. Many thoughts are possibly true but not necessarily helpful. Of course, we can't just block out every thought. However, consider how much headspace you want your unhelpful thoughts to occupy.

Most of the difficult outcomes we worry about will never happen or are incredibly unlikely. Instead, try to live in the moment whilst making realistic plans for the future. Planning too far ahead or worrying about unlikely outcomes can be very detrimental to our well-being and can rob us of enjoying the present. Worrying about the future casts a shadow over the here and now. Each day is a gift; try not to ruin today because of something that will probably never happen tomorrow.

Psychologists have coined the term *catastrophising* for a type of thinking pattern that predicts (often incorrectly) negative consequences and eventual outcomes. Catastrophisers play an imaginary chess game in their heads, imagining worst-case scenarios for every situation. They often have underlying anxiety and worry, or they may have experienced significant trauma in the past, making them more prone to think and expect the worst. Unsurprisingly, this can consume considerable mental energy and make them even more likely to feel fearful and anxious.

Unfortunately, life isn't perfect and bad things do happen, sometimes awful ones. Sometimes, it becomes apparent that something negative is about to happen. Worrying in these moments is natural, but it won't make you feel any better or change the outcome. Consider whether you're worried about something you can change (your score in a test) or something you have no control over (the results of a medical examination). Consider whether there's something you can proactively do to improve the outcome. If there is, take all reasonable measures to find a solution to the problem. However, if the problem is fixed and unchangeable, then dwelling on it's unlikely to be helpful as you can't change the outcome. Instead, try to accept the situation, make the best of it and find practical support to help you through it. Whatever your religious beliefs, the serenity prayer is a valuable way to approach these challenging moments in life:

Grant me the serenity to accept the things I cannot change, the courage to change the things I can, and the wisdom to know the difference.

HOW TO OVERCOME UNHELPFUL THOUGHTS

1. RECOGNISING UNHELPFUL THOUGHTS

How can you recognise when a thought is helpful or unhelpful? Helpful thoughts build us up, empower us to make positive changes and make us feel happier. They are our dreams, our positive self-talk and our inner reflections. These thoughts help improve creativity, increase our happiness and keep us hopeful for the future. Dwelling on these types of thoughts helps to strengthen our self-belief and gain a positive perspective on life. Some examples of helpful self-talk include *'I can cope'*, *'I've got the inner strength I need for this'* and *'I'm enough as I am'*.

Unhelpful thoughts, conversely, don't lift us up or inspire us. Some examples of unhelpful thoughts include *'I can't do this'*, *'I'm a failure'* and *'I'll never be good enough'*.

Table 8 helps you to recognise unhelpful thoughts. You can follow these steps:

1. Write down some negative or worrying thoughts.
2. Decide how likely these events are to happen and score the probability from one to ten.
3. Reflect on whether there's something you can do or change to improve the situation.

Table 8: Overcoming unhelpful thoughts

MY NEGATIVE THOUGHT	HOW LIKELY IS IT TO HAPPEN ON A SCALEOF 1–10? (10 being most likely)	WHAT CAN I DO ABOUT THE SITUATION?
I may fail my maths test.	6	Think more positively and practise more! Only watch one episode on Netflix tonight and do more revision instead.

You'll probably notice that most of the events you're worrying about are unlikely to happen. You can use Illustration 2 to help you consider if your thought is helpful or not; this is based on the likelihood of it happening and the control you have over the outcome. If an event is improbable, then the best action is to work on replacing the thought with something more helpful and positive based on reality.

Illustration 2: Are my thoughts helpful or not?

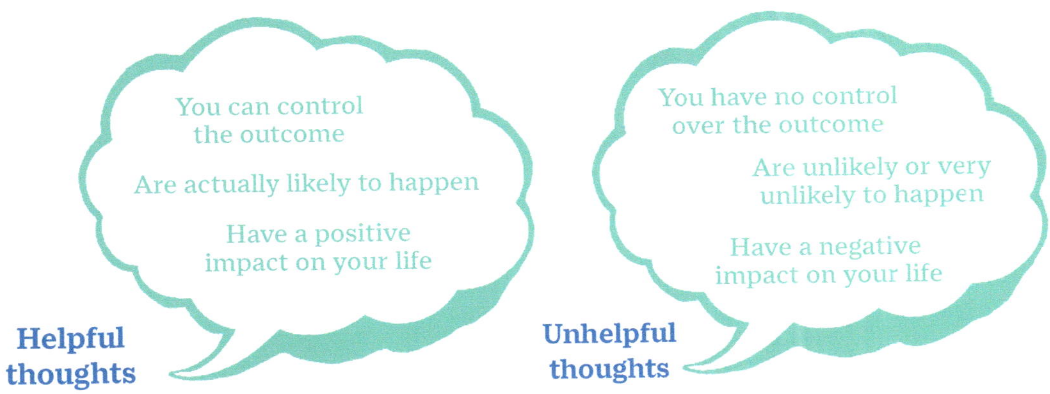

2. REPLACING UNHELPFUL THOUGHTS

Once you've recognised unhelpful thoughts (especially those where you have no control over the outcome or that are improbable), you can use the following techniques to replace them:

- Instead of dwelling on an unhelpful thought, try to think of an alternative, constructive action that you can change.
- Spend your time preparing practically to improve the outcome rather than just worrying about it; for example, revising more for a test you're worried about.
- For things you can't change, seek advice and support to find the best way to cope.
- Build a good support network of people that you trust.

Illustration 3: How to process an unhelpful thought

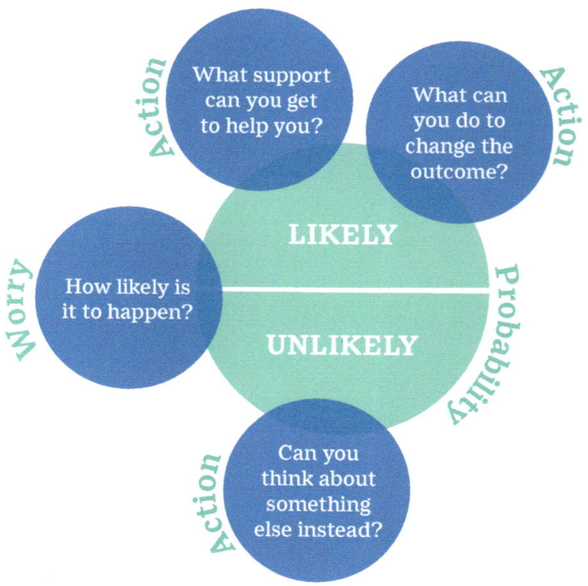

Grant me the serenity to accept the things I cannot change, the courage to change the things I can, and the wisdom to know the difference.

CHAPTER 6

GROWING YOUR MINDSET

Jess was bullied at school. She felt alone, unliked and left out. She didn't like studying, so in her spare time she turned to social media. Jess spent up to nine hours a day scrolling Insta and TikTok. Social media was the one place she could escape reality. She became so addicted to it that she would refuse to eat unless she had TikTok playing at the meal table. However, the more time she spent on social media, the less motivation and energy she had to pursue her dreams. She spent more and more time in her room, and less time studying. She saw other people's success on social media, and it made her feel worse about herself. She believed other people were more successful than her and felt she was a complete failure. Her mindset became very fixed, and she believed 'I can't do anything' and 'I'm useless at everything'. She dropped out of sixth-form college and started working in a café.

With the help of counselling and medication, Jess has turned a corner. It started with her changing her view of herself. With the help of her counsellor, she realised there are things she 'could' or 'can' do and would even be good at. Her mindset shifted from 'There's nothing I can do' to 'Perhaps there are a few things I'm good at'. She even managed reduce her social media and now only allows herself two hours a day. Jess recently looked after her little cousins and realised that she really enjoys spending time with small children. This has led her to enrol on an early-years course and she's even made some new friends. She's feeling much more optimistic about the future.

MINDSET

Have you ever wondered why different people have such different attitudes and outlooks on life? Some people appear open, optimistic and resilient, while others are more negative and afraid of failure. How we view our place in the world is called our mindset. It's a set of internal beliefs about our inbuilt abilities (for example, how clever or sporty we are) that dictates how we think, feel and behave. The beliefs we hold about ourselves subconsciously underpin our outlook on life and our coping skills, and this can profoundly affect all areas of our lives.

Professor Carol Dweck has shown that the key to success isn't about our actual underlying abilities but our beliefs about our ability to succeed. [36] According to Dweck, our mindset can predict our future success in life and our ability to overcome setbacks. She describes two ways we can view our inborn abilities:

- **Fixed mindset**: People with a fixed mindset believe their abilities are inborn, fixed and unchangeable. For example, if you have a fixed mindset, you may see failure as evidence that you're not good enough, or believe where you are now will predict where you'll be in the future. Unfortunately, when people with a fixed mindset experience failure, they can easily get stuck. They see failure as a sign that they lack ability and talent and think therefore they might as well stop trying in the future.
- **Growth mindset**: People with a growth mindset believe their abilities can be developed and strengthened through commitment and hard work. Having a growth mindset is about choosing positivity and effort over negativity and failure. Those with a growth mindset believe they can change their circumstances through hard work and don't let temporary failures set them back. [37] A growth mindset can lead to increased effort and more sustained achievement. For example, when faced with a problem such as trying to find a new job, people with a growth mindset have been shown to have greater resilience. They're more likely to persevere in the face of setbacks, whilst those with a fixed mindset are more liable to give up. Having a growth mindset helps us to believe in ourselves and to believe that we can find solutions to the problems we face.

Illustration 4: The difference between a growth and a fixed mindset

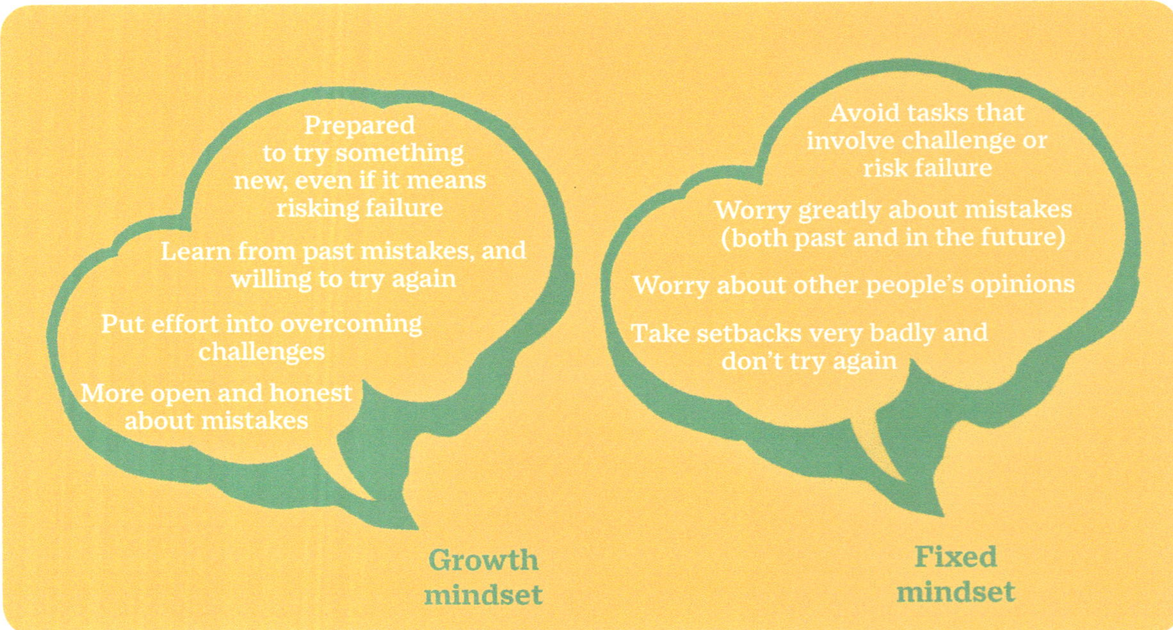

FACTORS THAT INFLUENCE OUR MINDSET

Many people use the glass half-full/half-empty analogy. When you look at a half-glass of water, do you see it as half-full or half-empty? If you see your glass as half-full, you may have a more growth-type mindset. The glass half-full represents your ability to see the positive in every situation and believe you have enough inner resources to make the difference needed. However, people with a fixed mindset see their glass as half-empty; they don't believe they have enough (both internal characteristics and external resources) to cope with challenges or create change. They think that they can't change, even with increased effort, and that effort doesn't make a difference to the outcome.

Social media can influence your mindset. As we've seen, a growth mindset is about believing in your own ability and strength. Spending time on social media can impact your belief in your own ability. It can externalise how you view yourself, making you dependent on other people's perspectives and comments (which may not always be positive). This can mean you stop believing in yourself and rely instead on other people's opinions. It can also make you feel powerless if you're constantly viewing the lives of other people who appear more successful or happy than you. Your mindset can become fixed if you stop believing in your own ability to change your situation.

Illustration 5: How growth and fixed mindsets impact outcome

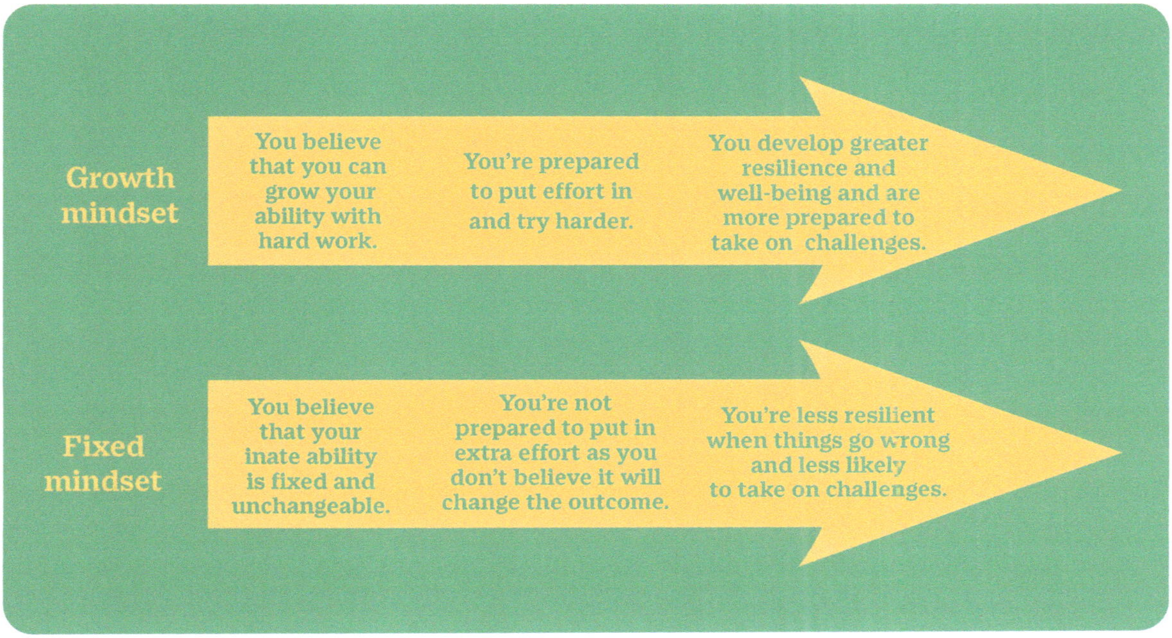

THE PITFALLS OF A FIXED MINDSET

Which mindset do you think you have? Can you see different areas of your life where you operate in a fixed or growth mindset? Do you have a fixed mindset in some areas but a growth mindset in others? Most of us have a mixture of growth and fixed mindsets in different areas. For example, you may believe you've never performed well in school so you will always *struggle* academically (fixed mindset). However, because you *excel* in sports, you feel able to improve and grow in the area (growth mindset).

This view may mean you put all your energy into sports but don't pursue your studies (as you don't believe you're any good, or that your hard work won't pay off as you're not clever enough). Or when it comes to exams, you might believe you'll succeed if you put in enough work (a growth mindset); however, with making friends you have a fixed mindset, thinking, *'I'm not likeable. I never make friends. I don't understand people.'*

There are six common thinking patterns that can hold you in a fixed mindset in specific areas of your life: [38]

- Black-and-white thinking
- Valuing success over effort
- Perfectionism
- Catastrophising mistakes
- Finding negative feedback difficult
- Competitive comparison

The following sections explore these fixed-mindset thinking patterns. As you read, consider whether any of them ring true for you. They may not all be relevant, but perhaps you can see where a few of them are holding you back from your healthy selfie. You can have a growth mindset overall, but there may be specific scenarios where your mindset is fixed. Recognising where and when you're operating in a fixed mindset can help you shift into a more growth mindset and move forward. Remember, the goal is to *like* and believe in yourself, inside and out.

1. BLACK-AND-WHITE THINKING

Luke had always been the best at hockey at school and in his county club. He was captain of the first team and one of the best county players. Hockey had been his life throughout his childhood. Luke went to university believing he was an excellent hockey player and tried out for the university team. He expected, unreservedly, to get into the first team. It devastated him when he only made the second. The standard of university hockey is incredibly high and very competitive. However, for Luke, making the second team was a devastating failure. Rather than seeing it as an incredible achievement and setting himself the realistic goal of making the first team another year, he gave up hockey altogether. He interpreted being placed in the second team as a sign he was a complete failure and useless at hockey. This then spiralled into negative self-talk about all aspects of his character and ability, and eventually led to a profound period of depression.

Black-and-white thinking is a type of all-or-nothing thinking pattern; for example, that you *can't* do something or you'll *never* be able to succeed. This thinking style is underpinned by the belief that your talent and intelligence are fixed. It can be a positive (you believe you're the best) or negative (you think you're the worst or incapable).

Unfortunately, either can set you up for failure. A person with a totally positive self-view may struggle when faced with a challenge, as they'll be surprised by how difficult it is. They may give up because of a false belief that because of their talent, everything should be easy. If a person innately believes they're the best, unique or superior, it will come as a shock if they don't come first or achieve the highest accolade. This causes disappointment and a sense of failure (even in the face of success). The important lesson is to believe in yourself whilst also acknowledging that success always takes effort.

> The key is to realise you can choose how to respond to obstacles. Life won't always be easy, but how you react to challenges is crucial.

On the other end of the spectrum, someone with a totally negative view of themselves may not even attempt a challenge. They might think they're stupid or not good enough, which means they won't try new things, thus perpetuating the cycle of failure. They may interpret one failed attempt as evidence that they're inferior and refuse to try again for fear of failure in the future. Being too hard on yourself might be your natural mindset or the result of years of criticism, but don't let it stop you from trying new things or putting effort into something you find difficult. Try reframing the way you think from *'I'm terrible at x'* to *'I might find x tricky, but I'll get better if I try hard'*.

I'm not naturally good at French. I'm highly dyslexic, which makes learning languages difficult (something I didn't understand until I'd left school). I spent my entire school career hating languages and feeling like a failure. Even numerous French exchanges were a disaster! On one, I misunderstood the instructions to pack for a week-long beach holiday and packed only a swimsuit and beach towel, thinking we were going on a day trip! I spent the entire week in the same clothes without even a toothbrush or spare underwear. Everything in me screamed that I was useless at French, a complete failure and should give up. Now, the reality was that I wasn't naturally brilliant at French, but I was - and am - pretty determined. I put a lot of hard work in and kept trying. I happily gave up French, but not before passing my GSCE French. I proved to myself that hard work and determination could be enough, even with little natural talent.

WAYS TO SHIFT A BLACK-AND-WHITE MINDSET:

- Try reframing the way you think to *'I will get better if I try harder'*.
- Don't let the fact that you find something hard stop you from achieving in that area.
- Focus on what you can do, where you can work harder and what help is available.

2. VALUING SUCCESS OVER EFFORT

This fixed mindset is underpinned by negatively viewing the need for significant hard work and effort. People with this mindset want quick results without putting too much in – they don't value hard work, but instead value success. This mindset can evolve through excessive success and praise at school or home that values *achievement* above *effort*. This can subsequently link achievement with reward and praise, and subconsciously couple effort with inadequacy. Low self-esteem often underpins this mindset because success is needed to bolster the person's view of themselves. It can become an addictive cycle, where they only feel good about themselves *if* they achieve.

Sometimes it's hard to succeed in the real world. This mindset can result in looking for success elsewhere, often in gaming or social media. Gaming is an example of where this mindset can thrive. Gaming has a high *reward-to-effort ratio*. Games are designed so that you always make progress relatively quickly, and your effort is quickly rewarded with success (going up a level, high scores, winning a game). You can put in hours of time and practice, which is rewarded by success in the game and an excessive release of dopamine (our feel-good hormone). This can lead to increased time gaming at the expense of time and effort in the real world.

In the real world, success can take much longer, is less obvious and is less dopamine-rewarding. It takes 16 years to get a GSCE, and hours and hours of practice to play a simple tune on an instrument. However, a growth mindset links your effort to success. It makes you believe that the more effort you put in, the more likely you will be to succeed. Remember 15-year-old me, who was finding French difficult? Despite lots of negative self-talk, I managed to reframe failure as an opportunity to prove myself. The lessons I learnt whilst passing my French GCSE, about myself and the importance of hard work and overcoming, have been far more important than the final grade.

WAYS TO VALUE EFFORT:

Practise putting effort in now. Rather than avoiding a subject or task you find difficult, don't be afraid to put the effort in so that you can improve. Doing this will cultivate a growth mindset and resilience, two tools that will be invaluable throughout your life.

If you find this difficult, here are some tips to help you:

- Don't give up if you find something difficult.
- Go back to basics and work on what you know and can do.
- Don't be afraid to try new things; it doesn't matter if you fail.
- Remember, your value isn't linked to your success.

3. PERFECTIONISM

Sixteen-year-old Jemma came to see me about self-harm and her persistent low mood. She had worked hard for her GCSEs and had done incredibly well. Jemma had scored all 7s, 8s and 9s, a tremendous achievement. However, she could only see the grades that weren't perfect 9s. Jemma felt like a failure and thought she could and should have done better. She couldn't celebrate her 16th birthday as she hadn't achieved everything she wanted to. Jemma saw all her hard work and sacrifice as wasted. She couldn't see that her ambition for perfect 9s was almost unachievable and that her marks were some of the best in her year group. She had fixed her mind on unachievable perfection and her exceptional grades didn't meet her expectations. Jemma was left with a sense of disappointment and inadequacy. Despite her incredible achievement, she spiralled into a very dark place.

Perfectionists set themselves exceedingly high goals and targets which are almost impossible to reach. With this fixed mindset, they view scoring anything less than 100% as a failure – perfectionists always focus on the few marks they've dropped in a test or essay. This can leave them feeling that they haven't done well enough or that a score isn't good enough. This sense of failure (despite success) can lower self-esteem and self-worth, thus perpetuating the cycle. Perfectionism is often an attribute of very high achievers, and it leaves them unable to celebrate their success. They'll always see their tiny mistakes, leading to overachievement and burnout.

Social media appears to contribute to perfectionist traits. Other people's 'perfect' lives are visible for all to see and can leave perfectionists comparing themselves to unachievable benchmarks.

Social media rewards people with a seemingly *perfect life* (especially external attributes) with *likes* and followers. It has created a powerful (but incredibly detrimental) scoring system based on popularity and success. There are substantial social and peer pressures around the use of

Illustration 6:The cycle of perfectionism

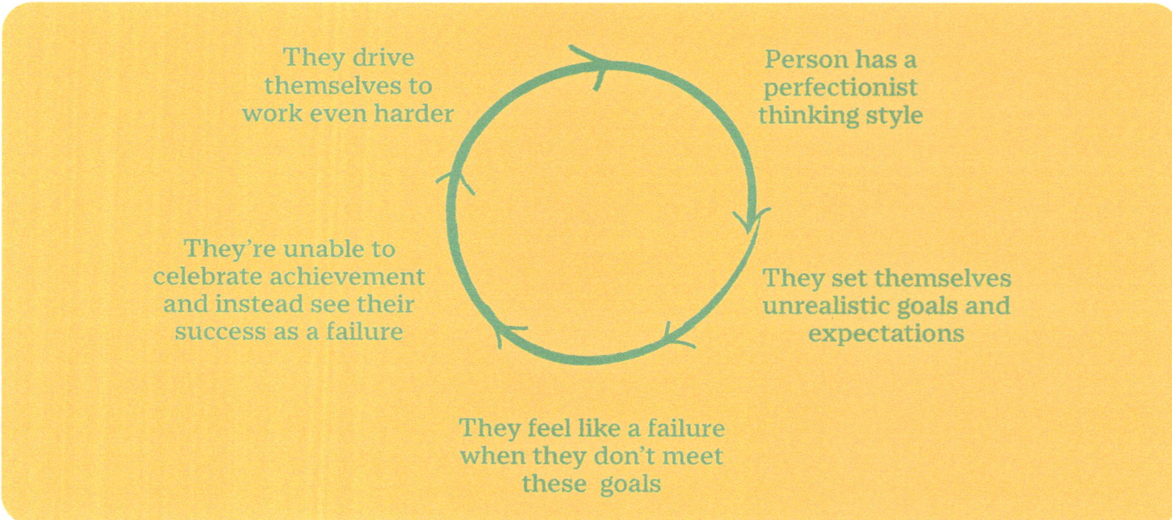

social media. Recent research has found that 90% of 12- to 15-year-olds who used social media said they felt pressured to be popular on these apps. [39] The need for popularity on social media can directly affect how someone feels about themselves. It can play into low self-esteem, thus perpetuating the cycle of needing to achieve 'perfection' in order to feel better about oneself.

BREAKING FREE FROM PERFECTIONISM

If you tend to be a perfectionist, try to gain a more balanced perspective about yourself. You can break the perfectionist cycle by setting realistic goals and working on non-linear targets (for example, being kind or enjoying a non-work-related activity). Attempt to tolerate lower-than-expected scores and results in all areas of your life; don't see them as a failure but as an opportunity for growth. Aim not to allow external-scoring systems (either test results or *likes* on social media) to dictate your life and value. Your likeability and lovability aren't based on being perfect; they're based on you being you. Be kind to yourself and try to like yourself more.

ASK YOURSELF THE FOLLOWING QUESTIONS:

- Is less than 100% a failure when the pass mark is 80%?
- Does my essay have to be word perfect, or can it be just good enough?

- Will spending hours in the gym make my body perfect, or is being healthy more important?
- Is comparing myself to Photoshopped models a good use of my time?
- Do I base my value on test results or social media *likes*?
- Does it help or hinder others if my life appears perfect (especially if it's not)?

4. CATASTROPHISING MISTAKES

How do you feel when you make a mistake? Do you see mistakes as a disaster or catastrophe, even if the error itself is small or inconsequential? Can you bounce back quickly, or does a mistake set you back and take ages to recover from? When you make a mistake, does it trigger feelings of low self-worth and low mood? Once you've failed at something, do you avoid repeating that activity? If you've answered yes to some of these questions, it may be worth considering your mindset in the area of your response to mistakes.

A person with a fixed mindset towards mistakes will misinterpret any mistakes they make to mean they're not good enough, or a failure. They're then likely to avoid similar challenges in the future because they become afraid of making further mistakes. Again, keep in mind that you don't see others' mistakes online; you see only their successes and achievements. It can completely skew your view of what 'normal' life is with ups and downs, boredom, normality and repetitive failings. If you view the online world as the benchmark for your own life, you'll find normality, let alone failure, very hard to accept.

On the other hand, a person with a growth mindset is more likely to view a mistake from a more positive viewpoint and try to learn from it. Mistakes are best viewed as an opportunity to grow, as we can learn from them and do things differently in the future.

Imagine how these two different mindsets can determine how you interpret a lower-than-expected score in your mock GCSE. A person with a fixed mindset may interpret the low score to mean they can't do it and give up trying. They may end up doing worse in their final exam. However, someone with a growth mindset won't necessarily view their low score as a failure, even if they feel disappointed. Instead, they see it as an important opportunity to improve and do better the next time. Mistakes made in practice papers can help highlight areas of weakness to work on in the future. They can help you improve your score in the actual exam. You're better prepared for the real exam *because of* your past failure.

Another example: imagine these two different mindsets in action over failure at a job interview. The person with a fixed mindset who doesn't get the job they really wanted may interpret this reaction to mean they're not good enough and not try for a similar job again. However, someone with a growth mindset may choose to receive (and learn from) the feedback from the interview and then look at ways to improve for the future. The next time a similar job comes up, they may have filled any gaps in their knowledge or experience and go on to successfully get the job.

CHANGING THE CATASTROPHISER'S MINDSET

Many of the world's greatest inventors, explorers and entrepreneurs have failure and setbacks woven into their backstories. It's not their difficulties that have defined them but how they used their failure to grow, develop and ensure success in the future. Bear Grylls, the famous TV adventurer, broke his back in his early twenties while parachuting with the British Army. He used this defining moment not as a catastrophic failure but as a pivot point in his life. It redirected his path and future. He used his recovery as a catalyst, which led him to be the youngest British man to climb Everest and return alive. He was just 23. His story, which you can read in his book *Facing Up*, is about overcoming adversity and not giving up. [40] He didn't give up after a huge physical setback that shattered his life dream of a career in the Army. Instead, he redefined his whole life in a new and powerful direction. If you can change how you view your mistakes, you can transform your story.

REFLECT ON A RECENT MISTAKE AND ASK YOURSELF THE FOLLOWING QUESTIONS:

- How can I learn from this situation?
- What can I change that will help me do better next time?
- How can I challenge myself to try again, and what support can I put in place to change the outcome in the future?
- How can I reinterpret the mistake without putting myself down?

Illustration 7: How different mindsets view mistakes

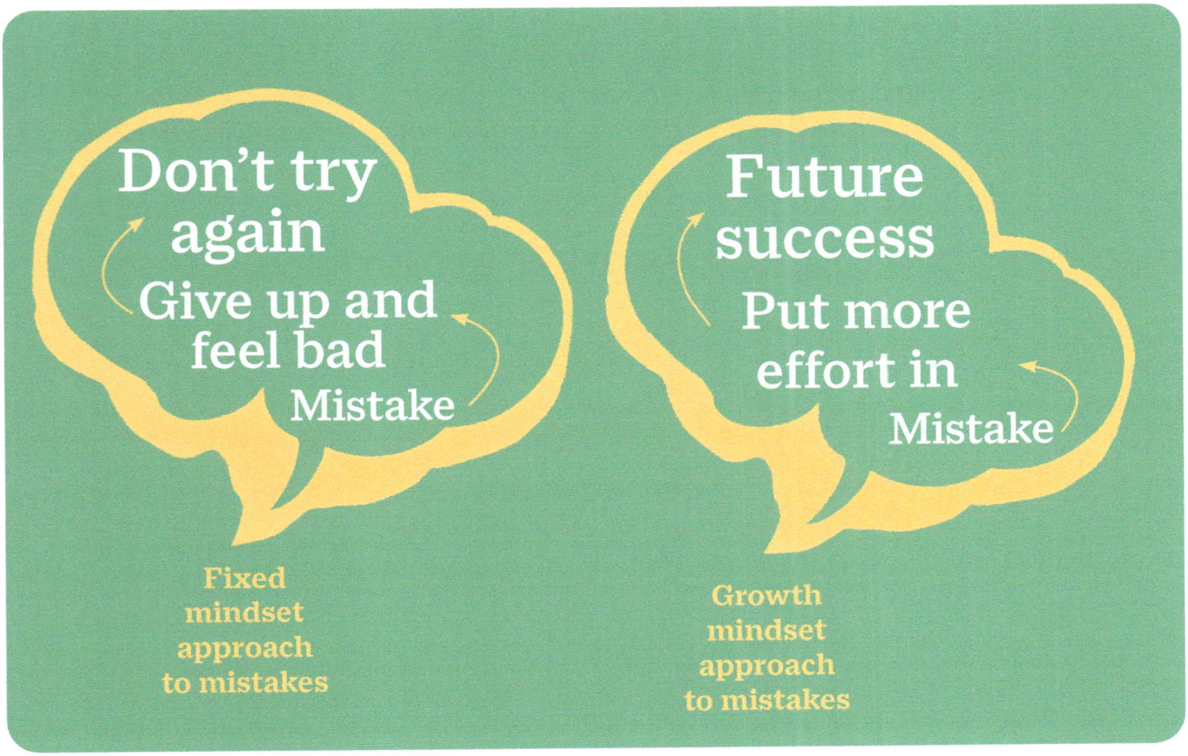

5. FINDING NEGATIVE FEEDBACK DIFFICULT

Imagine Harry, a 13-year-old boy, who was given a low effort and achievement score for his first term playing rugby. He had a fixed mindset and interpreted the grades to mean that he was terrible at all sports. As a result, Harry gave up his preferred sport, football, in favour of computer gaming, where he felt successful and less criticised. However, he never fully recovered from the sense of failure and loss of opportunity.

Whether or not you like it, negative feedback is part of life.

We all, at times, face criticism! Criticism can come from your parents, teachers and peers. It can even come from people you don't know – or don't know well – online. Sometimes criticism can be fair and at other times unfair (as is often the case with online comments where people have less of a filter on what they say).

Feedback can be positive or negative, and both kinds can help us to learn from our mistakes or successes and help us to grow. However, if misinterpreted, negative feedback can make you feel inadequate and useless. Think of the last time you received criticism. How did it make you feel? Were you able to reflect on the comments impartially, or did it trigger an overwhelming feeling of failure in you? Have you ever noticed you have an out-of-proportion response to negative feedback? If criticism sends you into a downward spiral, it may signify that you have a fixed mindset in this area.

Our ability to handle criticism is based on our underlying mindset. You may have a fixed viewpoint towards criticism that makes you see negative feedback as inherently wrong, and to link the criticism to failure or a personal attack, rather than seeing it as an opportunity to grow in an area (where you may be weak). A growth mindset view can change how you see criticism and turn it into something positive. Rather than seeing negative feedback as a sign of failure, a growth mindset enables you to sees others' views as valuable resources and an opportunity for growth.

Imagine the same 13-year-old Harry with a different mindset. In this scenario, he interprets the criticism in the context of being a new rugby player. He recognises where he hadn't tried particularly hard as he found it challenging. In response, he seeks to put more effort and practice into rugby. With this new attitude, he enjoys rugby more and performs well in the football season (where he's chosen for the first team).

HOW TO HANDLE CRITICISM

Try to see it as advice rather than criticism and reflect on what changes you can make in the future.

If you're unsure if the complaint is fair, check this with a friend or family member to see what they think. Choose someone whose opinions you trust. Don't race to send an angry email or text; think about what's been said, talk the situation through with a trusted friend or mentor, and consider an appropriate response. If the criticism still feels unfair, it may be relevant to feed your thoughts back gently, or it may be better for you to move on.

Illustration 8: A growth model for handling criticism

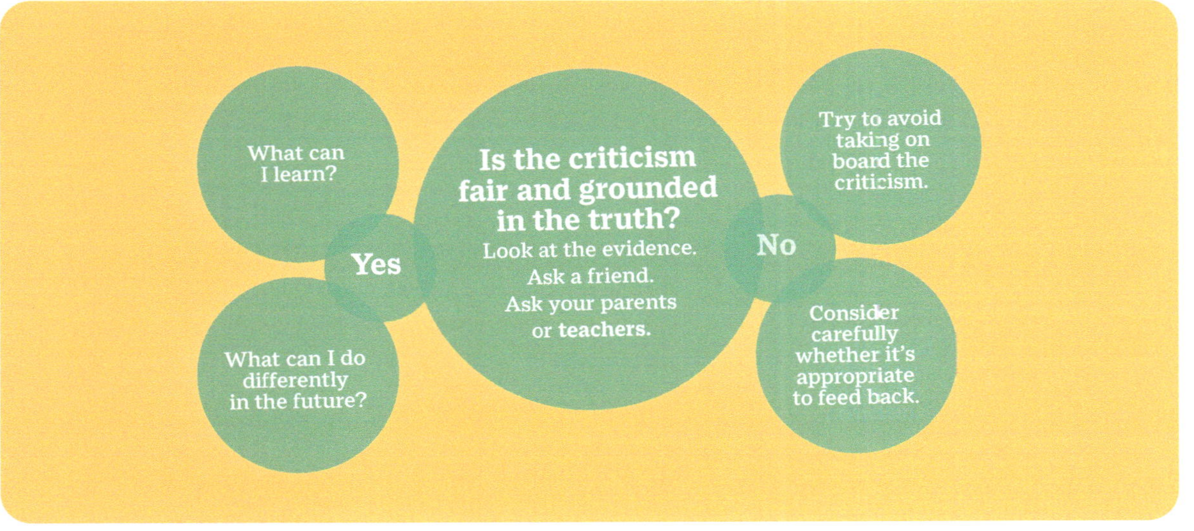

6. COMPETITIVE COMPARISON

A person with a fixed mindset in the area of comparison will compete competitively with their peers. Comparing yourself with others can be unfavourable (viewing others as better than you) or favourable (viewing yourself as better than others). Either way, other people's success may be difficult for you if you have a fixed mindset towards comparison. In unfavourable comparison, you compare yourself negatively to others. This can make you feel inadequate and not good enough. Comparison can occur in real life and online; you may compare your results, looks or achievements to your peers at school, college or online. Unfavourable comparison can leave you feeling frustrated and empty. It rarely motivates you to change, but instead lowers your self-esteem and well-being. On the other hand, if you already feel better than your peers and compare yourself favourably, others' failures can make you feel superior. This is equally unhealthy and can give you a false sense of pride and achievement.

Challenge yourself to put more effort into your personal development or goals, regardless of what others achieve.

Illustration 9: The impact of competitive and constructive comparison

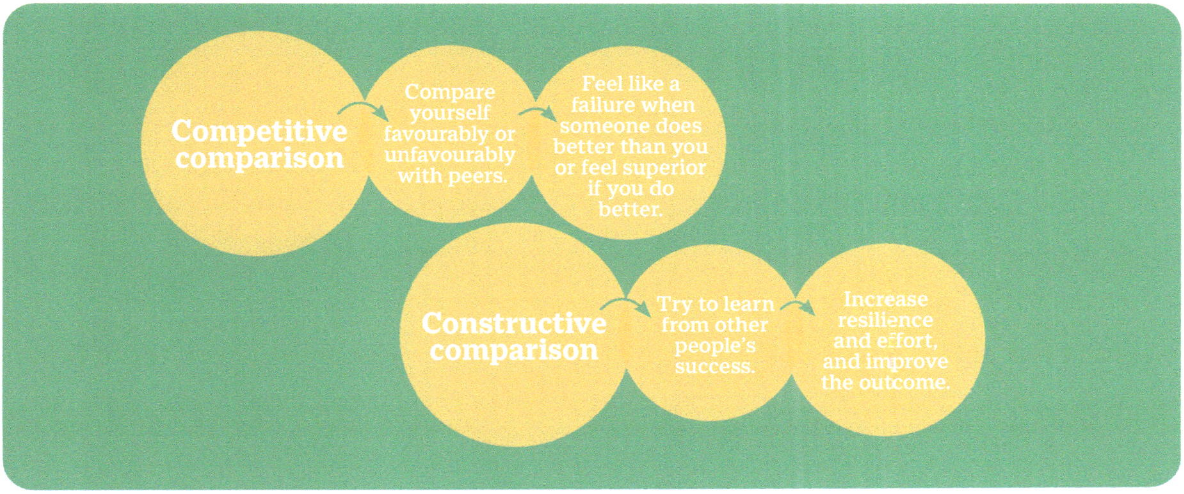

HOW TO USE COMPARISON CONSTRUCTIVELY

If, instead, you adopt a growth mindset, you can assess yourself based on your own goals and results. Setting goals focused on effort rather than just on accomplishments enables you to develop your growth mindset and motivate yourself to try harder.

Another powerful tool to overcome competitive comparison is to instead use comparison for your personal growth and development. Rather than looking at others' achievements and feeling inadequate, instead reflect on their accomplishments constructively. [41] Challenge yourself to put more effort into your personal development or goals, regardless of what others achieve. This attitude can help grow resilience, and although this isn't primarily about achieving more, improved outcomes inevitably follow an increased effort. Whatever others may say, very few people can achieve good results without hard work.

QUESTIONS TO ASK YOURSELF:

- What can I learn from other people's success?
- How can I use their success as an opportunity to grow?
- How can I prevent their success from making me feel inadequate or jealous?

HOW TO DEVELOP A GROWTH MINDSET

Unfortunately, you can't just change your mindset in one leap; you need to work on smaller steps first. To develop your growth mindset, consider an area in your life that you'd like to change, improve or challenge. Within this area, choose a *growth goal* on which to focus. A growth goal is something you want to achieve or alter about how you behave or respond. A growth goal doesn't have to be a substantial life-changing one; it can be a small step that you build on in the future. For example, you may decide you want to increase your physical activity or improve your social life.

1. SET GROWTH GOALS

If you're struggling to think about where to start, you can use the circle of life in Illustration 10 to help you identify an area that you're less satisfied with and would like to improve. Once you've decided on an area, think of a goal within that area to set. For example, if you only score two out of five in the friends and recreation quadrant, you may decide to work on this area.

Illustration 10: Circle of life

On a scale of one to five, think about how satisfied you are with each of these areas and write your score in the box.

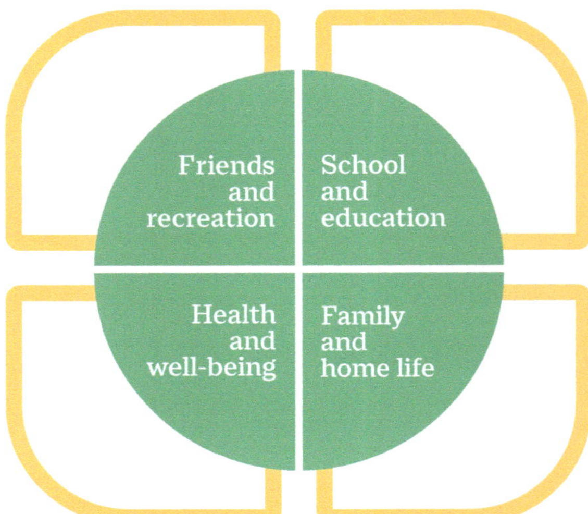

LOGIC TREES

The next step in achieving your goal is to break it down into smaller steps using a logic tree (see Illustration 11). The bigger steps (for example, wanting to improve your social life) can be broken down into even smaller steps (for example, joining a sports club or inviting friends to the cinema). In this way you break down what once seemed unachievable into achievable, more manageable steps.

1. Consider something you'd like to achieve and write it in the top box. Your scores in the circle of life exercise may give you a good place to start!
2. Use the flow chart to help you break down each element into smaller steps. Continue repeating the steps until you have a series of actions that you can easily undertake.
3. To reach your goal, start at the bottom step and work backwards towards your end goal. Regularly review the progress you've made towards your goal.

Illustration 11: How to use a logic tree

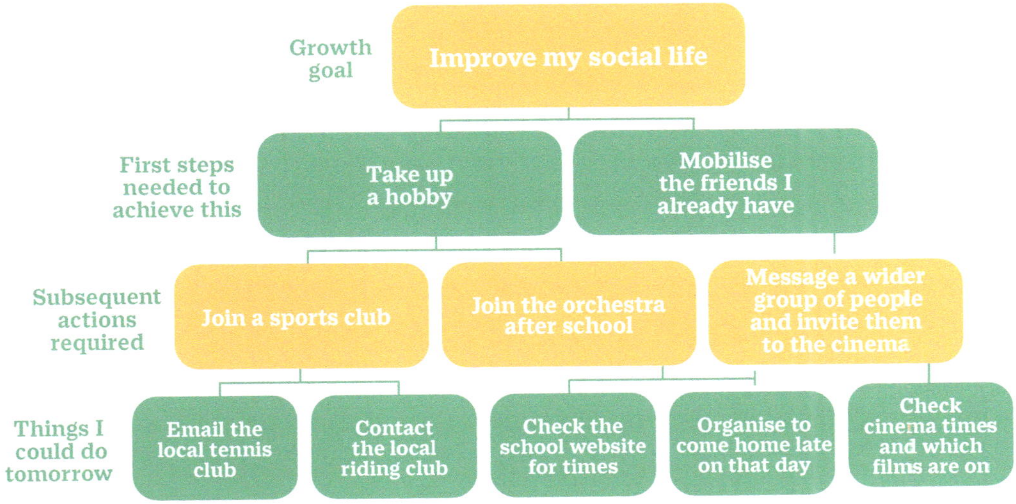

Adapted from *Techniques for Coaching and Mentoring.* [42]

Growth goal

First steps needed to achieve this

Subsequent actions required

Things I could do tomorrow

2. CHALLENGE YOUR OUTLOOK

Now consider situations in your life where you've faced challenges and assess whether a fixed mindset is holding you back. If it is, identify which of the six types of fixed mindset is at play.

Think of an alternative thinking pattern to offer a different perspective on the problem. Base this new thinking pattern on the growth mindset view that you can change most situations with hard work and effort. To help reach this change in viewpoint, you can set yourself a *challenge question*. This is a question that will help you alter your perspective in the area where you're stuck. Think about what's holding you back and what you need to do to overcome it. Viewing challenges in this way will help increase your sense of control over difficult situations. We saw in the self-esteem chapter (Chapter 3) that self-belief can help you feel empowered in the face of adversity, and it's a vital attribute of a growth mindset.

Table 9: How to grow your mindset

EXAMPLE OF FIXED-MINDSET SCENARIO	TYPE OF FIXED MINDSET	ALTERNATIVE THINKING PATTERN	CHALLENGE QUESTIONS
	• Black-and-white thinking • Valuing success over effort • Perfectionism • Catastrophising • Finding feedback difficult • Competitive comparison		What questions could you ask yourself to help move towards a growth mindset?
I'm going to fail my driving test.	Black-and-white thinking.	I'm making steady progress. I'm more than capable of passing my test.	What can I do to grow my confidence? What specific skills do I need to learn?

CHAPTER 7

BOUNCING BACK WHEN THINGS GO WRONG

Issy was a keen athlete; she loved the outdoors and was incredibly active. There was never a moment when she wasn't running, walking, or playing sports. Just before her 13th birthday, she started experiencing intermittent knee pain. Her knee looked normal, and it didn't stop her from doing anything, so she carried on as usual. Then, suddenly, on the last day of the summer holidays, her knee swelled up like a balloon. Instantly, she knew deep down that something was seriously wrong. After hours in A&E, she received worrying news: there was a large hole in the cartilage under her kneecap, and the doctors didn't know what was causing it.

Issy was fast-tracked for an MRI scan, which meant the doctors were worried about cancer. To Issy and her family's great relief, she didn't have cancer, but she had a significant cartilage defect in her knee. Because of its position, it was almost impossible to operate on. She was told that she would likely never return to any sport. She was given a pair of crutches and began waiting for surgery to remove the piece of damaged cartilage. The surgery would leave a large hole at the pivot point in her knee, likely affecting her for the rest of her life.

At this point, Issy began to despair. She put away her trainers, sports awards, and athletics kit. She watched movies and played board games. There were tears. However, Issy and her family didn't give up. The prognosis seemed too dire; there had to be a better way. Amazingly, her family stumbled upon a remarkable knee surgeon who was experienced in treating these rare and difficult-to-reach lesions. Within two weeks, Issy underwent open knee surgery to pin the cartilage back together.

The road to recovery has been incredibly difficult. However, Issy didn't complain, and she didn't give up. She focused on her physiotherapy and looked forward to her recovery. Bit by bit, albeit slowly, her knee improved. First, the crutches were no longer needed, then the painkillers, and gradually the swelling reduced. The journey isn't over, but Issy has shown incredible resilience in the face of adversity.

FACING HARDSHIP

Everybody has ups and downs in life. Sometimes things go well and at other times life is complicated, and at times it can even feel unbearable. You're not alone, unusual or unique if you face adversity; there's no way of avoiding upsets in life. Having a realistic view of life is essential in order to avoid constant disappointment, but this needs to be balanced by remaining hopeful and optimistic. This chapter looks at how to cope with challenges and bounce back when things go wrong.

Although every one of us will face difficult situations in our lives, it's important to recognise that the *share* of these difficulties isn't fairly distributed. Life is unfair and some people face far more challenges and hardship in their lives than others. But sooner or later, each of us inevitably faces at least one of the following difficulties:

- Failing at something
- Not getting picked for a team
- Doing poorly in an exam or essay
- Feeling ill, tired or low
- Having a friendship or relationship that fails
- Being criticised
- Making a mistake that we regret
- Experiencing someone we love getting sick and possibly passing away

I'm not trying to be negative! But it's important to be realistic. All these things will happen at some point in your life, and it's essential to be prepared, but without being worried or anxious. And remember, people are much less likely to share their negative experiences online, so it can make you feel you're the only one struggling. You can see it's a delicate balance between optimism and pessimism! Tip too far one way and you'll spend all your time (even when things are going well) worrying about what's going to happen in the future. On the other hand, if you're unrealistic and believe life will be (or should be) perfect, you'll have a horrible shock when something goes wrong! I don't want to rob you of youthful optimism, but I also don't want to set you up for a fall. In the middle lies a path with hope and purpose but one that's also realistic and grounded. That's where you want to be: *realistic hopefulness*. It's essential for your well-being.

THE IMPACT OF NEGATIVE NEWS AND DOOM SCROLLING

There are many, many things to worry about in our world today. We've all gone through a tough time in the pandemic, which has changed the way we see the world. Climate change is a real and worrying issue that's not going to disappear. War in Europe and the Middle East has erupted, probably something none of us thought we would see in our lifetime.

On top of all this, people are spending much more time online, scrolling through negative news (aka doom scrolling). You may have noticed once you start scrolling how easy it is to get lost in a rabbit warren of bad news. I've been there too! To my surprise, I realised that I'd developed a doom-scrolling habit; I could get lost online scrolling through negative news stories without even noticing. Even my sleep was affected because I was worrying about the stories I'd read.

It started during the coronavirus pandemic, when I wanted to stay up to date with the latest stories and statistics. I found that I quickly developed a habit of checking the daily Covid infection and death rates. Once online, I would get sidetracked by other negative feeds. Even after the pandemic improved, I found that my habit of doom scrolling had not. Despite my own best advice, I would check my news feeds before I went to bed and when I got up in the morning. But the news didn't make me feel happy or better informed. Instead, it increased my tendency to worry and distracted me from enjoying the moment. It's hardly a surprise that filling our brains with too much negative information doesn't make us feel good and, in fact, makes us less happy and more stressed. 'Being informed' can't change the outcome of world events and can make us less resilient to our own challenges.

So, as a New Year's resolution, I deleted the news app from my phone and I cut down on the news I read online. This definitely improved my mood. But I will admit, I may have substituted a weakness for doom scrolling with one for scrolling on Instagram (more on that later).

HOPE IN THE MIDST OF ADVERSITY

On a personal level, you may be going through a difficult time: your parents may have got divorced, or you may have lost a parent, or you may have experienced the horror of abuse, bullying, loneliness or ill health. However, amid the pain, there is hope. There's still goodness, love and kindness in the world (although at times it's hard to see). Good things can and *will* happen to us and to those around us. It's difficult, but try not to be overwhelmed by the negatives. Instead, focus on what you can do to make the world a better place and make thoughtful and hopeful choices in your own life. Be optimistic. Look forward. Make plans and believe in a better future. As you travel through life and meet challenges, remember that these are all part of your journey.

We all have different coping mechanisms to deal with setbacks, but the aim is to emerge more robust than we were before. Resilience is the ability to bounce back, recover and grow from a setback. It's about more than just returning to normal after a difficult episode; it's also the ability to learn from the process.

The key to resilience goes back to our mindset. Can we see life's challenges as an opportunity for growth? We develop resilience through experiencing adversity.

Unfortunately, we can't develop resilience without going through hardship. Adversity isn't the enemy, hopelessness is.

Navigation, learning from and overcoming difficulties are crucial for our future success and happiness.

SOCIAL MEDIA IS THE NEMESIS OF RESILIENCE

It may not surprise you that social media can be the nemesis of resilience. Social media conveys the message that life should be easy, perfect and beautiful. It teaches us that if our lives aren't perfect, there must be something wrong with us. Social media rewards portraying the perfect life over the imperfect reality (that life is tough). We don't receive *likes* for our difficult day, but for our filtered photos. This doesn't teach resilience. In fact, it teaches us the opposite and makes us feel alone or unique when things are difficult or we feel unhappy. This can contribute to mental health problems, as we're led to believe there's something wrong with us when we don't *feel happy* (like we see in other people's social media posts). Notice that we often project emotions onto other people's photos; for example, they're smiling and therefore they must feel happy. Remember, this isn't necessarily true. A smiling photo doesn't mean the person is feeling happy! It's very easy to post a happy selfie, but it's much harder to actually be one!

DEVELOPING RESILIENCE

The characteristics we need to be resilient are those we've already explored in this book. Growing your self-acceptance and self-esteem will give you a solid foundation for coping when things are difficult. A growth mindset will provide you with the courage and self-belief to navigate adversity. There's no magic answer, but a core belief in yourself and your coping ability is vital.

RETAINING HOPE

I got married at 27 to my wonderful husband, Hugh. Out of nowhere, four months later, I became ill. I remember vividly being on call at the children's hospital (where I was working as a junior doctor) when I suddenly felt hot, cold and achy. I thought I just had the flu. However, over the next few weeks, I became progressively more breathless. I'd been a marathon runner and suddenly I couldn't walk up a flight of stairs. Initial investigations were normal, as I still looked reasonably well on the outside. But I got rapidly worse and I was rushed into hospital with low oxygen levels a few weeks later. A CT scan showed extensive lung damage, and over the next few weeks, the doctors gave me a range of diagnoses and prognoses. None of them involved living for more than five years. Our hopes and dreams were shattered.

After some delay, the plan was to have an open lung biopsy so they could formally diagnose which life-limiting illness I had. I was admitted to the hospital and sat there with an oxygen mask, wearing only a flimsy hospital robe, awaiting my fate. I felt very vulnerable. I can't describe it, but in that moment of hopelessness, I chose to believe that whatever the outcome I would, and could, get through this, that there was an alternative and a better prognosis for me. I replaced fear with a glimmer of hope.

Two days after my biopsy, on a Sunday afternoon, I was lying very bruised and sore in bed with a chest drain in situ. I received a phone call from my consultant. The samples had been analysed, and contrary to what they'd previously thought, I had a reversible lung condition. It was a rare autoimmune disorder triggered by mould in our rented flat. I was treated with high-dose steroids and could breathe again within days. It wasn't an easy road to recovery; I had regular flare-ups and was on medication for several years. However, three years after my original illness, I had my first daughter and came off all medication. A few years later, I ran a half-marathon, albeit slowly. Apart from avoiding mould, I now lead a completely normal life.

That illness shook my worldview. It made me afraid that bad things really could happen. However, it also taught me hope and resilience. Even when awful things happen, there's a path through difficult times. You just need to find it.

Looking towards the future with positivity and having hope are essential to help us through more challenging times. Even in difficult times, there are always positives: support from friends, connection with our family, a greater understanding of ourselves, or just the fact we got through it! You may not be able to see it now, but things will get better. There is hope. And if you can't find hope yourself, allow others to hold hope for you until you can find it too.

KNOW YOUR ULTIMATE WHY

Meaning, in short, is the nourishing experience of feeling like we're connected to something larger than ourselves. It helps us thrive when things are going well, and it helps us cope when things go wrong in our lives. [43]

Meaning is about knowing your ultimate *why*. Finding purpose and meaning in your life can help give your life direction. The more challenging question is, *'How on earth do you find meaning?'*

Here's a question that young people are commonly asked but hate to answer: *'What do you want to do when you grow up?'* Knowing the answer is difficult! Many adults even struggle with the same question. It's hard to make plans for next week, let alone have a five-year plan mapped out. It's challenging to project forward and know what you want, let alone how to get there.

However, finding meaning doesn't have to be a big or scary task. It can simply be about understanding your value system and what's important to you. Once you know what's important to you, you can try to orientate your time and activities towards this goal. You don't need to know precisely what you want from life, but knowing what's important to you can help direct you. You'll find life more fulfilling as you spend your time and energy on what matters to you.

A core value is described as *'an enduring belief which influences and underpins the choices a person makes'*.[44] Knowing what your core values are will help you understand in which direction to travel. Values can be similar to our attitudes and beliefs but are longer lasting as they're more foundational. Over time, we can shift our beliefs, but we don't tend to change our core values. For example, we may have core values around creativity, physical strength and health, or love and relationships.

To explore your core values and discover what makes you tick, fill in Table 10. Rate the values from one to ten, with 'one' meaning it has little importance to you and 'ten' being the most important to you.

Knowing our purpose can help us get back on track when things are difficult.

Table 10: Core values quiz

VALUE	SCORE 1-10
Leadership	
Friendship	
Creativity	
Physical strength	
Curiosity	
Competence	
A comfortable life / financial resources	
Love	
Kindness	
Freedom	
Helpfulness	
Imagination	
Fairness	
Intellect	
Achievement	
Adventure	
Exploration and travel	
Honesty	
Wisdom	
Sociability	

Optimism

Loyalty

Patience

The well-being of my family

Bravery

Modesty

Independence

Liveliness

Organisation and order

Empathy

Gratitude

Adapted from a quiz created by the Berkeley Well-being Institute. [45]

Once you've completed the quiz, go through the list and highlight your top five values. Now list these in order of priority and you'll have discovered your top five core values!

MY TOP FIVE CORE VALUES

1)

2)

3)

4)

5)

When we start a journey, we need to know where we're going, or we'd just be driving around aimlessly forever. Once we know where we're going, we can then plan a route. We may get lost along the way, but all our subsequent choices will call us back towards our destination. Even when we're lost, we know where we're trying to get to. Google Maps goes into overdrive when we take a wrong turn. Every command tries to get us back on the right path, and the app isn't happy till we're back on the correct route.

> **Life is a journey in which we don't *exactly* know where we're heading. But knowing our core values can help orientate our lives towards our goals. It means we have a better idea of where we're trying to get back to when we take a wrong turn.**

Greta Thunberg, the Swedish climate activist, has inspired many of us with the way she's orientated her life towards climate awareness and action. It means all the choices she makes are orientated around this goal. It gives her great purpose and helps keep her focused. She knows her ultimate *why*, which is to campaign for climate justice. As a result, her time and energy revolve around this commitment.

Knowing your ultimate *why* can be difficult. Maybe you can think of some smaller goals that help keep you on track? Maybe you set passing exams as a growth goal in Chapter 6. I'd encourage you to look behind the dream; why do you want to achieve that? What are the core values behind it? Knowing our *why* helps keep us motivated. It helps us with decision making (which can be incredibly difficult) as we can orientate our choices towards that goal. It can help us with how we spend our time. I loved geography when I was at school and wanted to study it at A level. However, because of a timetable clash, I couldn't study geography *and* chemistry. I knew at this point that I wanted to be a doctor and needed chemistry A level to get into medical school. I dropped my favourite subject for the goal of becoming a doctor. This may sound obvious, but if I hadn't known the desired endpoint of the journey, I probably would have made a different choice. Knowing my ultimate goal helped me make a logical rather than a heart choice. When you're busy and struggling to fit everything in, ask yourself, *'Does activity x fit with my purpose?'* Having a context for our decision-making process is helpful. Knowing our purpose can help us get back on track when things are difficult. Like Google Maps, try to find the choices that lead you back to your goal.

ASK YOURSELF THE FOLLOWING QUESTIONS:

- What do I want to achieve? (Your aim.) For example, *I want to become a doctor.*
- Why do I want to achieve it? (Your motivation.) For example, *It's an interesting job that also has meaning.*
- What is my ultimate *why*? (Your purpose.) For example, *To help people lead healthier lives.*

Illustration 12: Know your ultimate ***why***

AIM
What do I want to achieve? ....

MOTIVATION
Why do I want to achieve it? ....

PURPOSE
What is my ultimate why? ....

CHAPTER 8

REAL RELATIONSHIPS

Libby was struggling with loneliness and isolation. She had friends at school, but they rarely met up at the weekends. She said she tried to make plans with them, but when she did, they were then very often cancelled by her friends at the last moment. She recounted numerous times she was all ready to go out, only to receive a snap *at the front door cancelling her. She told me it was as if no one wanted to be the first to commit, for fear of putting themselves out there. However, cancelling left her lonely and isolated with only her phone as a substitute to connect her to the outside world.*

REAL CONNECTION

We're all designed to need human connection, and this is especially important during adolescence. It's a period of intense change, uncertainty and misunderstanding, and some of the most powerful tools you have in your mental-health toolbox are your friends and support network. Real connection and relationships come through shared experiences of life's highs and lows. Friendship can take months and even years to grow, and is founded on shared experiences, interests and trust. Going through a difficulty with a friend can be powerful time to forge a deeper relationship, as it helps grow understanding and connection. Having trusted friends in our lives is a bit like having a safety net. They can catch us when life feels like it's in free fall. Likewise, being a trustworthy friend for someone going through a hard patch can bring us a sense of purpose and meaning.

Healthy relationships are an essential foundation for our well-being. Authentic connections with people who know and understand us can make us more resilient. Connecting with your parents (albeit in a different way to your friends) can also grow your self-worth and resilience. It may not always feel like it when they're nagging about homework or complaining about clothes on the floor, but they're on your side. They may even be able to help you.

When working at a university health service as a GP, I often spoke to students who didn't want to tell their parents how they were feeling (many were experiencing serious mental health issues). When I asked why, the answer was almost always that they didn't want to let their parents down or they didn't want their parents to worry about them. However, this meant they couldn't access their most significant support network, their parents and family. It meant that they faced their challenges alone, believing that their parents' love and support were based on their success. The vast majority of parents, though, are desperate for you to let them in.

> Don't be afraid to share your struggles.

You're not letting anyone down if you're having a difficult time. You don't need to be perfect to be loved.

True failure is, in fact, hiding our difficulties and pretending that everything is okay when we actually need help and support.

CONNECTION IS KEY

Being liked and accepted is an important part of adolescence, and it's no surprise that in today's technological age, social media is often the tool to facilitate this. Social media is becoming the primary way people connect and communicate with each other. This isn't necessarily a bad thing! It's fun, and most importantly, it gives you instant access to people all around the globe. However, what is its impact on your real-world, face-to-face relationships?

Remember Jess from Chapter 6, who spent nine hours a day online but didn't have a support network in real life, or Tia from Chapter 4, who compared herself to others online? Social media had a directly negative impact on both of their lives. Sometimes, lasting relationships are forged on the internet, but online friendships seldom replace face-to-face connections. Social media is most effective when used as a tool to build genuine relationships that also play out in the real world. The reality is that many online connections stay only in the cyber-sphere. Undoubtedly, mutual support, empathy and advice can be found on online platforms. However, this online support needs to be paralleled with real, face-to-face friendship.

The truth is, you can spend hours a day on your phone but have few face-to-face relationships to trust in real life. You may have multitudes of followers who see your workout routine, where you go on holiday or even what you ate for breakfast, but perhaps no one knows how you're really feeling. Social media can play on your fundamental need for relationships, affirmation and connection, but it rarely helps you develop deep and meaningful relationships. A recent survey found that: *'16-24-year-olds are the loneliest group in society'.* [46] The findings of this survey are quite surprising, as most people associate loneliness with the elderly, rather than young people. It also poignantly found that having more friends on social media was linked with a higher chance of loneliness in real life. Loneliness is the opposite of connection; it's that gnawing, empty feeling of being on your own, with no one to turn to. So important are friendships and relationships to well-being that studies have shown loneliness is actually bad for the health of adolescents, whereas friendship improves happiness. [47]

Consider why you spend time on social media. One of the top reasons may be to connect with people or to make friends. However, have you ever noticed that rather than fulfilling this need for connection, it can leave you feeling disconnected, isolated and lonely? It may also leave you feeling disappointed and dissatisfied, especially if you're having a difficult time and going online leaves you comparing yourself unfavourably with your peers or not receiving the affirmation you were hoping for.

EYE CONTACT

We've all seen people (or been that person) scrolling through their phone while ordering food, or texting during a coffee date with a friend.

> But have you ever stopped to think about the impact on your relationships of preferring your phone over the person in front of you?

Sometimes it might feel safer to look at your phone than to make eye contact, or it might seem easier to scroll than to engage in conversation. But what is the real impact on your ability to connect with others and feel like you belong? Think about how you feel when your friends don't make eye contact or speak to you because they're too busy scrolling. Have you considered how it feels for the coffee barista when a customer is more interested in their phone than in their order?

By intentionally (or unintentionally) disconnecting from the real people around you, you might be making yourself lonelier and harder to reach. Some of the best pieces of advice I've heard on how to avoid being distracted by your phone came from some students during my workshops. One girl told me that her family had no screens at the meal table, and if anyone broke this rule, they did the washing up. Another group of university students had a rule that anyone who checked their phone on a night out had to buy the next round of drinks. So, the next time you're tempted to pick up your phone, remember the importance of eye contact and try instead to put your phone out of sight.

FLAKY FRIENDS

As we've all become accustomed to people checking their phones rather than talking to us, so have we all become used to people cancelling plans. Cancelling has become more prevalent since Covid, but the seeds were planted long before Covid forced us to change our plans. 'Cancel-itis' – this tendency to cancel plans – has been growing over the past decade as ease of communication has increased.

When I was growing up, we only had a landline (closely manned by my father) and the Royal Mail with which to communicate, and it was therefore essential to be organised and reliable. I'll never forget a lonely Glastonbury Festival when I arrived at a designated meeting spot late and then spent most of the festival aimlessly looking for my friends in the crowds. However, pre-planning meant that an event would rarely get cancelled. With the shift that technology has brought, this is no longer the case.

The problem is, it's too easy: you can plan (and cancel) in a moment. However, the impact of cancelling at short notice on friendship, fun and connection is huge. Think back to a time when someone cancelled an arrangement you had made with them. How did it make you feel? Libby shrugged it off and accepted it as normal. However, underneath I could see it left her disappointed and frustrated.

All of us, whatever our age or gender, need friendship. Yet it can be hard to find. We need people we can depend on, who don't cancel plans for no good reason and will pick up the phone when we call. But instead we can end up with *flaky* friends: people who aren't reliable, who cancel and leave us hanging. The problem with flaky friends is that they make you vulnerable; they make you prone to disappointment, rejection and ultimately loneliness. For all its promise to connect us, social media can, thanks to the ease and anonymity of cancelling, actually keep us apart. You can end up substituting deep, meaningful connection with video Snaps and Instagram messages.

INTIMATE RELATIONSHIPS AND ONLINE CONTENT

Matty was ten years old when he first encountered porn accidentally online whilst doing his homework. What started as a quick peek to satisfy his curiosity quickly became a frequent habit. By his mid-teens, Matty was feeling flat and empty. He watched porn every day, sometimes multiple times a day. It left him with no interest in real relationships; he described feeling asexual towards women. Matty struggled to concentrate on his school work, frequently withdrew to his bedroom, and at times felt suicidal. He left school with few qualifications, and lacked any motivation for the future. He didn't realise it at the time, but many of his struggles were due to the violent and explicit porn he was consuming. Matty was profoundly depressed and couldn't form the relationships he really wanted. He came to see me in his early 20s as he was feeling so stuck and couldn't see a way forward.

It took a while before he trusted me enough to disclose his porn habit, which he then began to realise was having a profoundly negative impact on him. With help from a local support group, and after a few setbacks along the way, Matty was able to quit porn completely. The result was dramatic: his mood lifted and his motivation improved. He became interested in fitness training and subsequently got a good job he loved at his local gym. His interest in relationships and real sex returned and he met his now girlfriend.

Some of you reading this book will already be sexually active, while others will not be. All of you will be curious! Some of you may know your sexual orientation, and others may still be uncertain. While these individual characteristics differ for each of you, one thing is almost certain: you'll have been exposed (on some level) to sexual content online. You may have knowingly sought porn online, but many early encounters with porn are accidental. The average first exposure to porn is at age 12 while searching Google for homework. [48] But it's not just Google where porn can be accidentally found; often it's embedded in TikTok or Instagram feeds. While porn violates TikTok's and Meta's guidelines, their platforms are flooded with inappropriate content, and you don't need to spend long on it to view highly sexualised material. Some of the saucier reels are hidden by hashtags and filters. These are there to draw you in and often encourage you onto more graphic porn sites. There's currently no age verification for adult sites, and children as young as eight have been found to be accessing porn online. [49]

Not only does pornography create an unrealistic view of bodies, sex acts and relationships, but it can also make you feel less secure in yourself. If you have a porn-biased view of what you should look like and what sex should be like, you may miss out on the vital experience of discovery. Viewing porn can put huge pressure on you to experience sex in a certain way and make you feel inadequate. Early sexual encounters are often fumbling and messy! It won't be perfect. More important is to pursue a loving, consensual relationship where you can feel safe and secure and create shared experiences.

Pornography is becoming more graphic, more violent and more immersive. No longer is it just a still picture in a magazine; it's now nearly all in very graphic video format. Unfortunately, many of these videos portray sex acts that make people uncomfortable in real life, as well as sexual violence and non-consensual sex (sometimes with a minor). There's evidence that watching violent sex can change your attitude towards real-life sex. Studies have shown that watching porn can reduce sexual satisfaction and cause an increase in sexual violence. [50]

It may surprise you to discover that pornography use is associated with mental health problems, including loss of concentration, loss of motivation, low mood, insomnia and anxiety. It is often not until after frequent pornography users give up that they start to notice an improvement in multiple areas of their life, with symptoms they didn't even realise that pornography was contributing to. There can also be quite significant sexual arousal problems in heavy porn users, including loss of sex drive and problems with achieving erections. [51]

Watching pornography can also become highly addictive. You may find that the more you watch it, the more you *need* to watch it, and you may find you need to watch more graphic or violent material to feel aroused. Some people develop an unhealthy addiction to porn and find they need to watch it daily, or even multiple times a day. This is due to the fact that pornography stimulates vast quantities of the feel-good neurochemical dopamine in the reward centre of the brain, making you feel good and want more. Over time, you need more dopamine to stimulate the same response, something called tolerance. Frequent users of pornography may need to watch more pornography or more graphic pornography to achieve the same response.

Pornography has been likened to the addictive nature of cocaine, and studies have found similar changes in the brains of frequent porn users as in those of drug addicts. Researchers have made some insightful discoveries when studying heavy pornography users finding reduced grey matter and weaker brain responses when shown sexual pictures. These changes may be responsible for the fact that once you start watching porn regularly, it can be harder and harder to stop. [52]

It's normal to be curious about sex. Try to think carefully about what you view and how it may impact your sexual relationships and body image, both now and in the future. Remember, you don't have to watch pornography, even if all your friends are, and you also don't have to open or view porn sent to you via social media.

IF YOU WATCH PORN, ASK YOURSELF THE FOLLOWING QUESTIONS:

1. Do you feel pressured to watch sexualised content by peers and friends?
2. How does watching porn make you feel? Does any of it upset you or make you feel uncomfortable?
3. Is watching porn impacting other areas of your life? For example, is it coming before friends or hobbies? Is it impacting your relationships in a negative way?
4. Are you finding it hard to stop, or feeling compelled to continue?
5. Are you seeking out more graphic content to become aroused?
6. Is what you're watching/sharing illegal?

If you've answered yes to any of these questions, it's worth reflecting on your use of pornography and whether it's benefiting or harming you. There's a list of resources in the appendix to help you if you feel you've developed an unhealthy pornography habit.

TOXIC MASCULINITY

Toxic masculinity describes a pattern of male behaviour that's being promoted and normalised on the internet. It's a version of masculinity that requires men to be tough, aggressive and strong, in control and wealthy. No one portrays this more than the social media celebrity Andrew Tate. He's risen to huge fame with over 12.7 billion views on social media despite being banned on nearly all platforms. [53] Tate idealises a showy and pushy form of masculinity based on wealth, power, sexual promiscuity and luxury cars. Tate promotes their use for his *own* control and gain, both financial and sexual. And this is where the problem lies: toxic masculinity promotes a shallow and selfish approach to manliness that doesn't take into account the feelings of others or the need for mutual respect or long-term purpose. For many young men what Tate offers may look great on the outside (fame, women and wealth), but it comes at the cost of your moral compass and the ability to hold down a loving relationship.

In recent times gender roles have become less clearly defined, with responsibilities at home and the workplace now shared more equally between men and women. Whilst breaking down gender stereotypes and role models has brought new freedom for both sexes, it has also made it more complicated to understand the true meaning of modern masculinity. In this confusing environment, the pushback towards toxic masculinity can *appear* attractive. Andrew Tate offers easy answers and a sense of vision and purpose. [54]

However, there are lots of ways to be truly masculine that still support the well-being of others and the development of mutual love and respect in relationships. By all means aspire to get fit and to be successful and decisive, but look carefully at who your role models are and what type of man you really want to be.

HOW TO FORM REAL RELATIONSHIPS IN THE DIGITAL AGE

1. DON'T BE FLAKY

Commitment and reliability are essential foundations of friendship. Whatever the social norm and etiquette, cancelling plans does harm relationships. You can try to create a positive culture in your friendship group. There'll be many times when you may feel like cancelling; you may be tired, feeling ill or anxious, or have lots of homework. However, within reason, I challenge you to try to keep your commitments. Most of the time you'll have a good time and be glad you went out. The more you go out, the easier it becomes.

2. MAKE EYE CONTACT, NOT IPHONE CONTACT

It's so easy to get lost in your phone during a meet-up, but remember, giving someone your full time and attention matters. Try to show your friends and family how important they are by being fully present. It may feel difficult at first, but put your phone out of sight and focus on the person who's in front of you.

3. EMBRACE YOUR BODY

All bodies are different. No body is perfect. All intimate 'bits' are unique and no two people are the same. Please try not to compare yourself to the stars you see online as you will fall short. Intimacy requires vulnerability and embracing your unique self.

4. FIND HEALTHY WAYS TO EXPLORE SEX

Whether or not you watch porn online is a choice. Only you can decide. However, don't fall into the trap of watching porn because everyone else is or because you can't stop. There are plenty of healthy ways to learn about sex and relationships that aren't so addictive or destructive.

5. CHOOSE YOUR ROLE MODELS WISELY

The internet has allowed many people without any credentials to become famous. A huge variety of people now have an immense online audience and reach. As there are no rules or qualifications as to who has the largest audience, it's for us, the viewers, to consider the content we consume. Think carefully about the views of people you watch online, and if they're really who you want to *follow*.

6. POSITIVE MASCULINITY

I encourage you to focus on discovering what type of man you aspire to be. There are many excellent and admirable qualities in modern masculinity which I encourage you to discover and pursue.

USE THESE QUESTIONS TO HELP YOU: [55]

- Name five good qualities you see in yourself. How can you nurture them?
- What kind of man, partner and (potentially father do you aspire to be?
- Are you currently on track to become this type of man?
- If not, what changes can you make in order to become the kind of man you would be proud of?

CHAPTER 9

UNDERSTANDING STRESS

Alex was working towards his A levels. He'd done well in his mocks and had worked hard all of Year 13. He made sure he studied every evening and most of the weekend. He'd stopped playing football and had cut down on seeing friends and watching TV. Alex was determined to do well. However, over the year, he noticed he was struggling to sleep and felt increasingly edgy. He felt tired and irritable all the time and couldn't concentrate. The work continued to pile up and his grades began to drop. He became overwhelmed and felt that he couldn't go on. Instead of studying, Alex spent hours procrastinating and lying in bed on his phone. He found it almost impossible to get out of bed in the mornings and get anything done. Alex was suffering from stress and burnout.

FIGHT, FLIGHT OR FREEZE

The *stress response* is the body's way of adapting to danger and improving performance when encountering a threat. Brief bouts of stress can help focus the mind and improve concentration. The body releases stress hormones from the oldest part of the brain, the limbic system. It's called our *fight-flight-or-freeze response* and it primes our bodies to react to a threat (either to run away, to stay and fight, or as a last resort to freeze and play dead). Adrenaline signals for blood to be sent to our muscles and for our heart to pump faster, while cortisol releases glucose into the bloodstream to sustain our energy levels. We're now ready to run, fight and survive!

However, too much of this fight-flight-or-freeze response can cause a long-term overproduction of adrenaline and cortisol (the body's stress hormones). This puts the body into a state of long-term stress, which can negatively impact our health, performance and well-being. Imagine if you spent weeks on end running from an imaginary lion. It would leave you feeling on edge, anxious and unable to sleep, as your body would constantly be prepping for a fight with no time for rest and recovery. The stress response makes you feel uncomfortable to warn you of danger (and help you avoid it in the future). Perhaps you know what that edgy feeling is like?

Some of the unpleasant feelings we may experience (feeling on edge, worried and tired) can affect our mood and well-being, as the stress response makes us feel awful. The stress response is quite simple. When we perceive danger, we release stress hormones, and these have an effect on our bodies. Until our bodies recognise that the threat is over, they will keep pumping out hormones, leaving us in an unpleasant state of stress. In today's busy, exam-driven, success-driven world, your body can falsely see almost anything as a danger or threat. Even the *thought* of certain activities or people can send your stress response into overdrive. Illustration 13 shows that what we think about subsequently impacts how we feel and therefore behave.

Illustration 13: Thoughts, physical feelings and behaviours when you're stressed

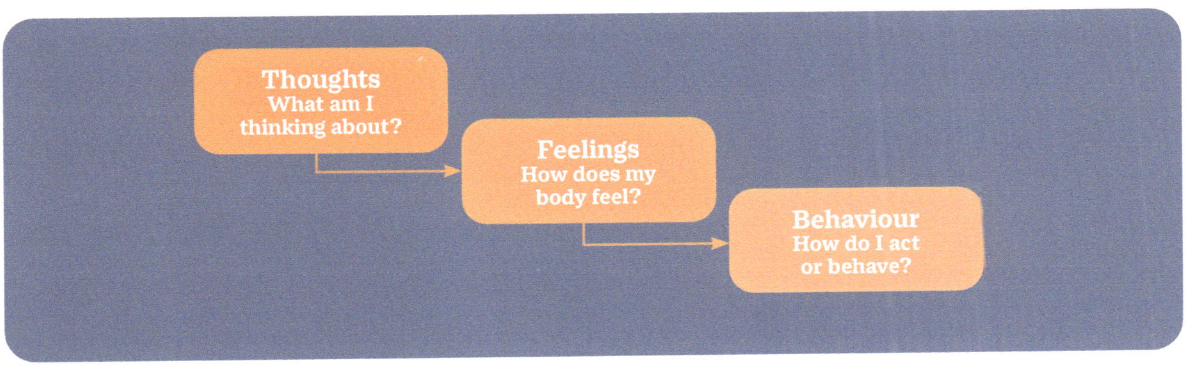

SOCIAL MEDIA AS A SOURCE OF STRESS

Social media (and technology in general) can directly and indirectly affect how stressed you feel. It's a subtle stressor, but there are numerous ways it may be impacting you:

- You may feel pressure to be liked and popular, and to post regularly and devote lots of time to crafting the perfect posts.
- Through social media you're much more aware of what your friends are doing and this can trigger FOMO (fear of missing out). You may notice all your friends are together on Snap Map or see photos of a gathering you weren't invited to.
- Being available 24/7 is incredibly tiring. Heavy social media users may feel stressed because they have less time to sleep and relax and are on constant alert for messages.
- As mentioned in Chapter 8, social media enables (often encourages) 'cancel-itis', where people cancel plans at short notice. Arrangements can also be made or changed in a snap, and this can leave you feeling uncertain and unable to prepare.
- As discussed in Chapter 7, doom scrolling can also trigger your stress response.

All of these individual 'stressors' are small. Therefore, you may not notice them. However, together they have a collective impact on how you feel. We all need rest and downtime. It's not a badge of honour to be connected 24/7 but feel stressed, exhausted and burnt-out.

These stressful feelings are often worse when you don't believe you have the inner resources to cope with the challenges you face. This again relates back to social media and the impact it has on your belief that you can cope. If you rely on other people's comments for your sense of worth and value, it can stop you from believing in yourself and your own abilities.

> No one is immune to stress. But we're better equipped to cope when we believe in ourselves.

SIGNS OF SHORT-TERM STRESS

Brief bouts of stress are unavoidable and can help with performing a skilled task - for example, exams or performing in front of people. However, too much short-term stress can cause anxiety and panic attacks. Here is a list of symptoms that you may experience due to short-term stress (please note that you may not experience every symptom):

- Heart racing
- Sweaty palms
- Breathing faster
- A feeling of impending doom
- Feeling on edge or more irritable than usual
- Panic attacks

SIGNS OF CHRONIC STRESS AND BURNOUT

Long-term stress can affect us both physically and mentally. It can cause *stress burnout*. Burnout is a state of physical and emotional exhaustion. We normally imagine burnout only happening to people with stressful jobs. However, such is the pressure on young people today and the impact of technology that it's occurring in young people as well. These are the symptoms of long-term stress. You may experience some or all of them:

- Feeling tired all the time, lacking energy and feeling exhausted
- A feeling of helplessness
- Feeling alone
- Having a negative and cynical outlook on life
- Avoiding hard tasks and procrastinating
- Feeling overwhelmed
- High blood pressure
- Poor sleep
- Weight loss or weight gain

Illustration 14: Understanding the stress cycle

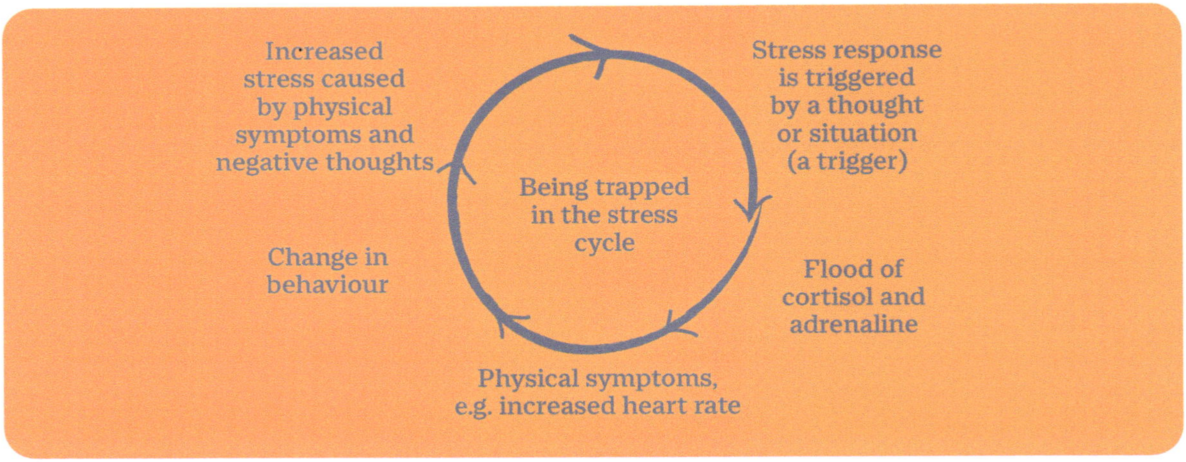

UNDERSTANDING THE STRESS CYCLE

Once your fight-flight-or-freeze response is triggered, you can become trapped in a cycle of stress hormones and subsequent behavioural changes, as shown in Illustration 14. Once you are in this cycle, your body needs to switch off the stress response in order to return to its relaxed state.

Think about how many people you know who are stressed. Are they constantly exhausted, overworked, tired and on edge? This doesn't have to be you. Let's look at what triggers your unique stress response, and then learn how you can turn it off again.

WHAT ARE YOUR TRIGGERS?

A trigger is any person, place or situation that activates your stress response. Triggers can be anything that subconsciously sets off our fight-flight-or-freeze response. For example, your trigger could be an argument with your parents, a big exam, a social situation, a difficult piece of homework or even a large spider. Remember, triggers don't have to be dangerous. Obviously, dangerous situations (correctly!) set off our fight-flight-or-freeze response, but the problem is that triggers can also be everyday events. Because life today is so busy, stressful and demanding, we can have a long list of triggers. Our brains are trained to remember what we've found stressful or threatening.

Spend the next few days learning to spot when your stress response is being triggered. In the first column of Table 11, write down the scenarios that triggered your stress response.

HOW DO YOU FEEL WHEN TRIGGERED?

In the second column of Table 11, write down how you feel and what you're thinking about when your stress response has been triggered. These could be physical symptoms: increased heart rate, sweaty palms, shaking legs, headaches, fidgeting or butterflies in your stomach. Or they could be psychological symptoms: anxious thoughts, overthinking, irritability, feeling powerless, a feeling that something is wrong, or questioning your ability to do something.

HOW DO YOU BEHAVE?

Finally, in the third column of Table 11, consider how you behave. During your moments of stress, how do you respond? Are you angry and irritable, or do you withdraw and sulk? Can you keep functioning, or do you feel so dreadful you have to withdraw? Does your stress response stop you from doing things and make you change your plans?

Take the example of my friend changing our carefully made plans at the last minute. Instead of meeting at the arranged destination, she asked me to make a significant detour to pick her up. This may not seem a big deal, but it triggered these thoughts: *'It will ruin our time.' 'We won't have enough time together.' 'She doesn't value me because she asked me for a favour.'* In terms of my feelings, I felt uncomfortable, noticed my heartbeat and felt more on edge. This affected my behaviour: I was edgier and snappier with my husband and children before school.

Table 11: Mapping your stress response

SITUATION THAT TRIGGERS MY STRESS RESPONSE	WHAT AM I THINKING?	HOW AM I FEELING?	HOW AM I BEHAVING?
I've had a big argument with my dad.	I'm worried that my dad doesn't love me anymore. I'm so angry with him for yelling at me.	My heart is racing and my hands are sweaty.	I'm hiding in my room; I don't want to talk to anyone.

The more you recognise your triggers, the more you can do something about them. The key is not to avoid them, but to train your body and mind to know that they're not dangerous. It may feel easier in the short term to avoid the things that make you feel anxious. However, rather than overcoming the anxiety, this results in your world becoming smaller, as you avoid more and more things.

RETRAINING YOUR STRESS RESPONSE

The aim is to recognise how you feel and think when you're stressed so that you can recognise the symptoms and de-stress more quickly. The following sections explain two steps that can help you manage stress:

1. Controlling your response to your triggers by reframing those triggers.
2. Turning off the stress response once your fight-flight-or-freeze response has been activated.

The goal isn't to eradicate all stress from your life, as that's unrealistic, but to learn how to avoid overreacting to stress triggers.

As a start, I encourage you to use the techniques in Chapter 11 to reduce your screen time. Try a digital detox or having some phone-free time, and I guarantee your stress levels will reduce.

1. REFRAMING YOUR TRIGGERS

First, you need to retrain your brain to recognise that specific triggers don't pose a threat or as serious a threat. Look at your triggering activities. The likelihood is that none are dangerous (although there may be a few exceptions if you live a risky or daredevil life!). For example, my trigger was a close friend changing our plans at short notice. The reality is that this scenario isn't dangerous and obviously won't kill me or ruin my life. At worst, it's an inconvenience, or possibly an oversight by my friend. However, my brain incorrectly recognised this as a *code-red, stressful life event*. This may be thanks to past experiences of last-minute plan changes that led to difficult outcomes or being late (something I hate). Or it may just be down to my need for control and organisation! Either way, my fight-flight-or-freeze response shouldn't have been activated. Seeing my friend is a happy, joyful event, not one to make me feel stressed.

Think about your own triggers. Try this exercise (adapted from a technique in Mark Schoen's book *Your Survival Instinct Is Killing You*):

1. Sit comfortably and focus on your breathing.
2. Think about your trigger.
3. Now think about a happy thought or memory.
4. Every time you experience this stress trigger, try to focus on the happy thought instead. [56]

Repeat this regularly and you'll find that thinking about the stress trigger automatically brings up your happy thought, not your stressful ones.

Table 12: Reframing your stress triggers

TRIGGER	STRESS-RELATED THOUGHT	ALTERNATIVE, MORE POSITIVE THOUGHT
I've had an argument with my dad.	My dad hates me. I'm awful. We'll never sort this out.	I'm sure he'll calm down eventually. We've argued before and we always make up in the end.

2. TURNING OFF YOUR STRESS RESPONSE

Once your fight-flight-or-freeze response has been activated, you need to do things that signal to your brain that you're safe again. This will help to stop your body releasing stress hormones and therefore turn off your stress response. It's not something that just happens – you need to engage in an activity that prompts your body to shift gear. [57] Here are six suggestions from the book *Burnout* by Emily Nagoski; try them and find one that works for you. [58] It's about finding the right activity for you that tells your body it's safe again. You need to discover *your* solutions to turn off *your* stress response. Only you, with your unique experience and makeup, can discover what makes you feel safe. Once you've found it, use it.

GET PHYSICAL

Physical activity is one of the best ways to turn off your stress response. [59] Any physical activity will do, but ideally choose something that gets your heart rate up. Thirty quick star jumps will help jolt your body out of its fight-flight-or-freeze response. I've always found running the best way to break my stress cycle. At times, I've run miles and miles. Currently, I run for 30 minutes around a few flat fields near to where I live. I burn off my stress, process my thoughts and emotions, and tell my body it's safe to relax again. My middle daughter, meanwhile, loves swimming. She goes up and down the lanes several times and comes out of the pool feeling happy – she's turned off her stress response. Others ride a bike, box, scoot, walk or play team sports. Find the exercise that suits you. Recognise what helps you the most and engage in that activity regularly.

What if you hate exercise? I feel your pain, and I'm not trying to dismiss your experience. However, if you can do some form of physical activity, however small, you'll feel better (I promise). Exercise can be gentle and fun – jog at a slow pace so you can talk with a friend while doing it or dance to some music in your room. Try to find an activity that you enjoy doing. Factor in regular exercise or physical activity to prevent stress from building up.

The goal isn't to eradicate all stress from your life, as that's unrealistic, but to learn how to avoid overreacting to stress triggers.

CONTROL YOUR BREATHING

Slow, deep and purposeful breathing can soothe your stress response. [60] Focus on drawing your breath in, holding it, and then exhaling a long, deep breath. A simple breathing technique is to breathe in for three seconds, hold for four and breathe out for five. [61] Repeat this exercise several times and see how you feel at the end. By stopping and focusing on your breathing for a minute or two, you can signal to your body that you're safe and that the danger has passed. You can also try meditation, yoga or Pilates - these activities help you to focus on and control your breathing, and they're really helpful for managing stress.

CONNECT WITH A FRIEND

Connecting with a friend is a beautiful way to change your body's stress response. Positive social engagement (aka friendship) can signal that the danger has passed and you're safe again. Social connection is usually a 'rest activity' and should signal to the brain that you're safe. Even when you're busy, have exams to revise for or have lots of homework, find time for your friends!

If you're feeling stressed, it might feel good to just send a quick *snap* or watch a few TikToks, but your mind and body need more than this. Instead, try to meet with friends in person regularly for fun and relaxation.

For some people (if they find friendships difficult or experience social anxiety), socialising may be one of their triggers. If that relates to you, work on the exercise earlier in the chapter (page 146) on reframing your triggers. In the meantime, use a different method to help you when you feel stressed.

LAUGH

> Laughter is another fantastic antidote to stress. Studies have shown that laughter triggers the release of our feel-good hormones called endorphins.

Endorphins interact with receptors in the brain and help relieve pain and trigger pleasure. One study concluded that: *'The pleasurable and calming effects of endorphins might signal safety and promote feelings of togetherness.'* [62] This is why laughter turns off your stress response – it fosters a sense of security and connection.

I came home from work one night feeling tired and somewhat stressed. I felt a bit on edge and was keen to get my children to bed so I could flop in front of the telly (please note, this is *not* one of the six ways to turn off your stress response, although it is good for relaxation!). My son found a sticker from some underwear I'd just bought. He stuck it on his forehead and walked around chanting, *'I'm part of the knicker deal.'* There was something in his carefree attitude that made us both laugh! Rather than hurry him up to bed, I enjoyed the moment of interaction and laughter. I turned off my stress response without even noticing and had a deep, restful night's sleep thanks to the knicker-deal sticker!

SEEK AFFECTION

Affection can trigger the release of oxytocin, another feel-good hormone, in the brain. Oxytocin stimulates the brain's reward pathways and makes us feel happy; it lowers our blood pressure and heart rate, and improves our mood. Oxytocin is released through physical contact with someone you love and trust. A 20-second hug can help break our stress cycle and positively impact our emotional and physical health. [63]

Have a 20-second hug with someone you love and trust. It must be a long, firm, safe hug to have the desired physiological effect. A 20-second hug signals we've escaped danger and arrived safely. We're now safe and secure. And better still, we're safe and loved.

After listening to wellness writer Emily Nagoski on a podcast, we started using the 20-second hug in our family to good effect. [64] When I'm feeling stressed, I pause and ask for a 20-second hug (or longer) until I feel better.

If you don't like hugs or don't have a suitable safe person to hug, cuddling pets is also great for releasing oxytocin and helping you feel safe. We have a therapy dog called Pippi for our middle daughter, who has severe anxiety and hates going to school in the mornings. She starts the day with a cuddle from Pippi, and instead of being flooded with her stress hormones, she experiences a burst of her happy hormone as the day begins.

If you don't have a pet and don't want or are not able to give a family member a long hug, then please consider one of the other ways to calm your stress response.

No one is immune to stress. But we're better equipped to cope when we believe in ourselves.

GET CREATIVE

For some people, creative expression is where they connect and de-stress the best. Whether through music, art, gardening, baking, writing or dance, being creative can have a remarkable effect on the brain. Creativity reduces our stress levels and allows us to enjoy a positive, calming practical activity. One study found that 45 minutes of creative activity significantly reduced stress in the body, regardless of artistic experience or talent. [65]Think about what you enjoy and what makes you feel good and spend more time on this activity.

RECOVERY

Finally, consider again the thoughts, feelings and behaviour you experience when you're feeling stressed. Rather than spiralling downwards, think about what you can do at each stage to break your stress cycle. Our bodies are not designed to be on high alert all the time. We need rest and sleep. Long-term stress can lead to anxiety and have long-term health consequences. Learning how to switch off your stress response will make you happier and healthier now and in the future. Take time to relax, and most of all try to find – and do – things that you enjoy!

Illustration 15: Changing your thoughts, feelings and behaviour

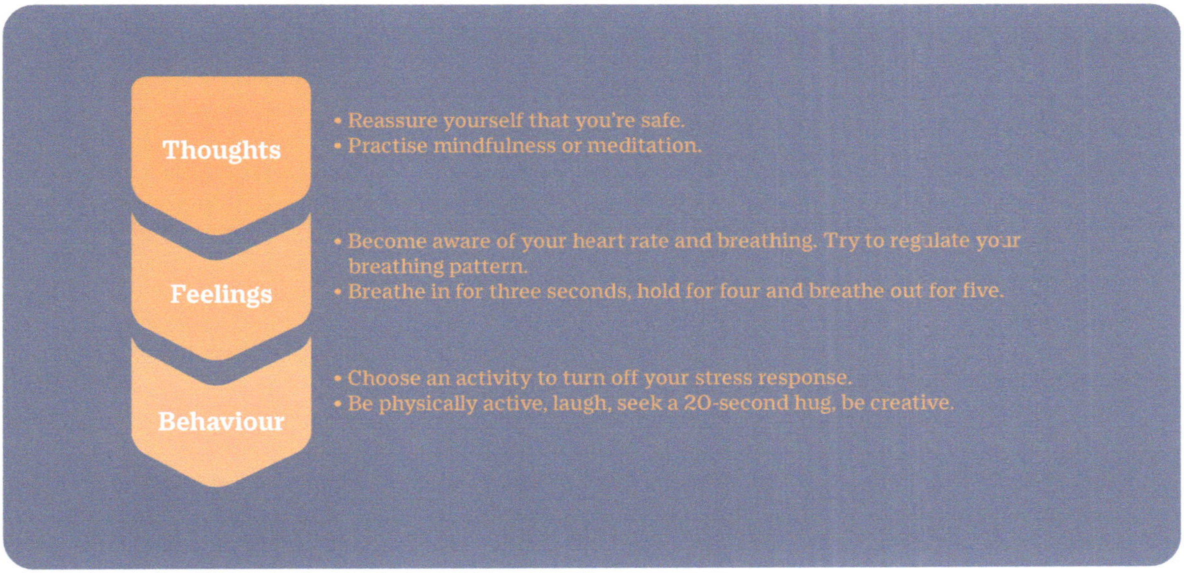

CHAPTER 10

WELLNESS

The Healthy Selfie wouldn't be complete without a chapter on looking after yourself physically as well as mentally. However, your journey to finding your healthy self will always begin where we began, with liking yourself. Adopting healthier lifestyle habits can make you feel much better physically and improve your sleep and energy levels, all of which provide a foundation for lower stress levels. But there's little point in adopting a super-healthy lifestyle if you can't like and accept yourself. Both super-healthy and unhealthy lifestyles can be driven by a lack of self-acceptance and low self-esteem, and as you work on growing these, your desire to look after yourself will also increase.

Don't worry about the unhealthy habits of yesterday. Instead, focus on what you can do today to improve your health and well-being. In this chapter, we'll look at how sleep, physical activity and diet can improve your health and wellness. This isn't about having a list of dos and don'ts (which can be very dull and disempowering, as it's impossible to follow all of them). It's about empowering you to make good choices because you like and value yourself. If you're still struggling with liking yourself, perhaps go back to the beginning of the book and redo some of the exercises there. If this still isn't helping, it's really worth booking an appointment to see your GP or seeking help from mental health charities.

HOW TO USE YOUR TIME WELL

Charlie was one of the students I helped while working as a university GP. He complained that he felt constantly exhausted, struggled to concentrate and experienced anger issues. The slightest problem would set him off in a rage, and this was adversely affecting his relationships. He requested an extension for his first essay, saying he couldn't focus and was having difficulty keeping up with his studies. When pressed, he disclosed this was partly due to his other commitments. He swam on the university swim squad, led the debating team and liked to game late into the night most evenings.

He recalled his childhood, which had been filled with rushing between various after-school clubs and training to becoming a professional swimmer. He swam at five a.m. every day before school, which left him tired, angry and exhausted in the evenings. Because he was frequently so tired, he didn't have the time or energy to meet up with his friends and felt isolated and lonely.

Charlie recognised that he harboured a significant amount of pent-up anger and frustration due to the lack of control over his childhood, which had mainly been dedicated to swim training. However, he felt unsure of any alternative way to live as swimming had been his focus for so long, even though he knew this lifestyle didn't make him happy. Over time, I helped Charlie recognise the importance of rest and he was able to make some significant changes to his life that made him much happier, including giving up pro swimming.

BUSYNESS AS A BADGE OF HONOUR

It's helpful to recognise where busyness and work can impede your self-care. In today's society, people often see busyness as a badge of honour. You can become so saturated in your busy life (school, homework, clubs, sport, screen time and socialising) that you can't see how little spare time you have. Making sure you have enough spare time and rest is essential to help you relax and turn off your stress response. Self-care and self-love start with giving yourself the time you need to look after yourself and engage in things you enjoy. Without rest, you may gradually perform less well, start sleeping poorly and eventually suffer from chronic stress burnout. A friend once told me she could tell how much a person liked themselves by how full their diary was! The fuller their diary and the less time they gave themselves to relax, the less she concluded a person liked themselves. I think she has an excellent point, although some people do thrive on being busy.

Keeping your life balanced improves your well-being, health, mood and sleep. There are times in life when it's impossible to avoid a certain degree of stress and busyness (especially around important exams or deadlines). However, even in the busiest periods, try to take some time off for yourself. Your stress response is less likely to be triggered in the first place if you're well rested.

TAKING MICRO-BREAKS

> The quieter moments of life - for example, waiting in the lunch queue or walking the dog - allow your brain little *micro-breaks*.

These micro-breaks enable your brain to switch off, daydream and rest. In the process, your body stops releasing stress hormones. The human brain and body are designed to relax (which is why sleep is so important).

However, the modern pace of life and constant technological connection can erode the natural inbuilt pauses in your day. So easily, your phone can rob you of these micro-breaks, allowing you to squeeze extra *snaps* or social media posts into these periods of downtime. It may feel efficient and entertaining, but it makes it much harder for you to switch off. You can be constantly in alert mode rather than in rest mode. This constant 24/7 brain activity means you continue to release stress hormones - which, as we've seen in Chapter 9, can increase baseline stress levels and worsen anxiety.

> It's impossible to quantify how vital these micro-breaks are for our well-being.

I'd therefore encourage you to run a mini experiment. For the next few days, decide not to check your phone in these little bits of downtime. Instead, focus on the moment, enjoy the view, focus on your breathing or think about something that makes you happy. Chat with the person next to you. Feel bored. Try using these quiet moments to relax. This will allow your body to rest and recharge, instead of continually pounding it with anxiety-provoking hormones. After a few days, reflect on how you feel physically (tiredness, aches and pains, heart rate and breathing patterns) and emotionally (mood, anxiety and general well-being). Do you feel better?

THE IMPORTANCE OF MARGIN

I often introduce the concept of *margin* to my patients to help them slow down and reduce their stress levels. We all have different capacities - i.e., how well we cope with lots of activity. Some people work well under pressure, whilst others work best with less stress. Neither is good or bad. We're all different. The important thing is to recognise our own capacity and how to keep within it. At what level of pressure can you function well without feeling too stressed? How much time off do you need to feel at your best? Are you a high- or a low-capacity person?

Once you've considered your ceiling, which is the maximum capacity you work well at, then try to introduce some margin. This means working at a level that's 10–20% lower than your ceiling capacity. It means not pushing yourself to the maximum all the time but giving yourself some breathing space. There's no exact science to this, and there is (to my knowledge) no precise measure of capacity. But try to get a sense of your limit (you'll know when you reach it, as you'll trigger your stress response), and then live your life under that limit! That means carefully considering how you spend your time and what you choose to say yes and no to. Self-reported data from Childwise found that 7- to 16-year-olds who went online spent 3 hours 48 minutes a day online on average. This equates to 26 hours 36 minutes a week of your spare time on screens. [66] Much of life may feel out of your control (school, family commitments and homework), but there'll still be lots of things you *can* control, especially your screen time.

The idea of margin is to not push yourself to your absolute limit all the time. There may be times before exams or when you're working on something important that you sacrifice some of your margin to achieve the task. It's okay to push yourself in the short term. However, margin is essential for your health and well-being in the long term. Margin allows you to switch off your stress response.

To introduce margin in your life, try giving yourself more time to complete activities and more time between activities. That way, you won't be rushing from A to B, and the whole process will be more enjoyable. Try overestimating the time something will take and enjoy the spare time that this allows if you finish sooner than expected. Before saying yes to something, consider whether you actually have time to squeeze it in. What impact will it have on other activities or your energy levels? Consider saying no to things you don't realistically have time to do.

HOW TO INTRODUCE MARGIN

The following exercise is designed to help you reflect on how you spend your time and how healthy it is for you. Using coloured pens, fill in Table 13 with your activities over the next week. Colour-code each section as follows:

- Use red for an activity you found unenjoyable or energy-draining. Red activities will be different for everyone. Remember that what's exhausting for one person may be restful for you and the opposite for others. Red activities will vary extensively depending on whether you're an introvert or an extrovert. The critical question is, *'How does the activity make you feel?'* If it's something you don't look forward to and that makes you feel drained afterwards, it's probably a red activity.
- Use orange for a neutral activity, something you neither especially enjoyed nor disliked. These activities are energy neutral and tend not to be the ones you worry about beforehand. Again, they'll vary extensively depending on your personality and what you enjoy doing. Examples may include doing your homework, going to school or doing chores.
- Use green for activities that were energy-restoring and fun, enjoyable and refreshing. Examples may include meeting a friend for coffee, going to the gym, reading a book, talking to a friend on the phone or listening to music.

At the end of the week, notice which colours are most prominent. If it's mainly red and orange, that may be an indication that your week was too busy, which may have impacted your well-being. Or you may notice that your week was unbalanced, and that there were pressure points in the week; for example, lots of red activities on one particular day.

Table 13: Colour-code your diary, Week 1

	MORNING	AFTERNOON	EVENING	NIGHT	HOW I FELT
MONDAY					
TUESDAY					
WEDNESDAY					
THURSDAY					
FRIDAY					
SATURDAY					
SUNDAY					

Check your screen time: .... hours a week

How I felt at the end of the week ....

YOUR NEXT SEVEN DAYS

Once you've completed seven days of colour-coding, think ahead to the coming week. Think about the activities you have planned and what colour they are. Aim to reduce, where possible, the number of red activities, whilst increasing the number of green activities. Try to have at least one green activity every day, even if it's only for ten minutes (but aim for a minimum of half an hour). Consider switching your weekly activities around to make the week more balanced, or dropping something to give you more time for green activities. Be mindful of how long you are spending on your devices and aim to reduce this. Rather than filling your spare time with screens, focus on activities that improve your well-being. Now fill in Table 14 to record your week in colour.

Table 14: Colour-code your diary, Week 2

	MORNING	AFTERNOON	EVENING	NIGHT	HOW I FELT
MONDAY					
TUESDAY					
WEDNESDAY					
THURSDAY					
FRIDAY					
SATURDAY					
SUNDAY					

Check your screen time: .... hours a week

How I felt at the end of Week 2 ....

If you felt an improvement in your well-being after changing your schedule, consider trying to make these changes permanent, and be mindful of your activities and how they

HOW TO SLEEP WELL

Sapphire came to see me because she was having trouble sleeping. She explained she felt tired and depressed, and lacked any motivation. She was only getting a couple of hours of sleep a night, which made her feel awful in the daytime. Sapphire had tried various remedies such as hot baths, herbal teas and over-the-counter medications, but unfortunately, nothing seemed to work.

It transpired that because she found it so hard to sleep, she would try to distract herself with her phone. She spent hours scrolling, and when she finally drifted off, she would be woken up by phone notifications. She felt compelled to check the messages as she didn't want to miss out on the chat overnight, leading to more scrolling before she eventually drifted off again. She was trapped in a cycle of not sleeping at night and napping in the day.

THE IMPORTANCE OF SLEEP

I'm sure you already know that sleep is essential to our well-being. At some point, every one of us will have had a terrible night's sleep. And we all know how horrible we feel the day after a broken night! But worse than one bad night is a run of awful nights, with endless hours of tossing and turning and the impending worry about feeling exhausted the next day. Sleep deprivation is linked to mood swings and irritability. It even makes us more prone to disorders like anxiety and depression.

The exact purpose of sleep is still a bit of a mystery to scientists. Contrary to what most people believe, sleep isn't resting time for the brain. Instead, current research points to sleep being a time when the brain processes waste products (toxins from chemical reactions formed when we're awake). It's also an essential time for processing the day's activities and laying down new memories. [67] Sleep is a restorative process that's essential for energy levels, concentration, reducing stress and boosting our immune system. [68]

DARKNESS AND THE IMPACT OF SCREENS ON SLEEP

Good sleep is, therefore, vital - but unfortunately, it's not guaranteed. There's no automatic switch to turn it on at 11 p.m. That's because sleep is a natural response to neurochemical (hormones in the brain) and environmental triggers. Environmental factors that impact our sleep include our stress levels; how much exercise, sunlight and fresh air we've had that day; our caffeine intake; and how we spent our evening. Our bodies need the right environmental clues at bedtime to know it's time to switch off. We also require the right environment during the daytime to be ready to sleep later on that evening. The body has a unique internal clock, including a day and night rhythm called the circadian rhythm. A particular part of the brain (the supra-chiasmic nucleus) controls it. Unlike a clock, it relies on environmental stimuli to keep it on time. Light and darkness are crucial to keeping the clock working. Darkness triggers the release of a particular sleep hormone called melatonin. Melatonin tells our bodies it's time to sleep.

We've seen how the sleep cycle depends on environmental factors, especially darkness, to trigger the sleep hormone melatonin. The sleep cycle evolved before artificial light was invented and it hasn't been able to adapt to new light-emitting technology. Smartphones and tablets emit a particular wavelength of light called blue light, which blocks the sleep hormone melatonin. Even glancing at our phone at 10 p.m. can confuse our brains and impact our sleep cycles. Studies have shown that if we use social media at night, we'll have poorer sleep quality, lower self-esteem and greater levels of anxiety and depression. [69]

REST, ROUTINE AND YOUR SLEEP CYCLE

Ironically, *rest* is essential for sleep. As we've discussed in Chapter 9, we release the go-faster hormone cortisol when we're stressed. Cortisol acts to wake our bodies up and blocks our ability to fall asleep. Think about giving yourself more rest (or margin) in the daytime. Rest allows us to turn off our stress response and helps us feel more relaxed.

By 'rest' I don't mean napping! Spending the correct amount of time in bed is important; this means not napping in the daytime or having a long lie-in. Reducing your time in bed helps create a sleep drive in your body - a strong desire for sleep.

It's also very important to make sure you're winding down in the evenings to prepare your body for sleep. Winding down prevents your mind from racing at bedtime, one of the main reasons you may find it hard to sleep. Thinking about your day or worrying about tomorrow or how long you've been awake can prevent you from falling asleep. Think about a new evening routine that helps you wind down (including trying to avoid screens). [70]

If you struggle with sleep (insomnia) and suddenly try some good habits for a few nights, it often won't work straight away. It will take several weeks of persistently good sleep habits (sleep hygiene) to reset your body clock. So don't give up if things don't change overnight. You can retrain your brain with good sleep cues, which will eventually reset your body clock. It may take changes to your relationship with food, the outside world and your screen to shift your sleep pattern.

TOP TIPS ON SLEEP

1. ROUTINE

- Keep to a regular bedtime and wake-up time. Sleep is rhythmical, and keeping a routine is one of the best ways to encourage a healthy sleep pattern.
- Avoid daytime naps or going to bed too early before you're tired.
- Fresh air, daylight and exercise during the day help you sleep at night.

2. DE-STRESSING BEFORE BED

- Try not to turn sleep into a big deal, as the fear of not sleeping can further provoke anxiety. Reassure yourself that nothing awful will happen if you have a poor night's sleep.
- Practise making space for downtime in the day to reduce stress and cortisol build-up. If every minute of the day is filled with school, screens and homework, it's not surprising that your brain can't instantly switch off at bedtime. Try a short period of relaxation in the afternoon - for example, colouring, listening to music or ten minutes reading a book - instead of filling every moment with busyness and stimulation.
- Try not to work late into the evening (remember, we need sleep to enhance our memory and store what we've learned that day).
- It's a good idea to avoid exercising and watching scary films late at night.
- Keep a notepad by your bed to write down anything you're worrying about. Once your worries are on the list, try to forget them until the morning. Remind yourself they're safely on the list and therefore you won't forget them.

- Focus on happy, positive thoughts at bedtime; for example, focus on something from your day, however small, that you're thankful for.
- Consider some of the old-fashioned favourites for aiding sleep: a hot bath, hot milk and lavender.

3. REDUCING SCREEN TIME BEFORE SLEEP

- The best advice is to not use smart technology for an hour before bed. Ideally, don't have screens in your bedroom at all.
- You can lower the blue light emitted on your phone by changing the settings or using a filter. You can also wear amber glasses to block the blue light. However, any smartphone use is stimulating (even without the blue light issue) and will tell your body to wake up.
- Use an alarm clock so you don't need your phone in your room.

4. GET THE ENVIRONMENT RIGHT

- Make sure your bedroom is dark and the right temperature (neither too hot nor too cold), and that your bed is as comfortable as possible.
- Avoid caffeinated drinks like Coke and coffee, and Pro Plus supplements (ideally after 1 p.m. as caffeine stays in your system for up to eight hours).

Don't give up - rebuilding your brain's sleep rhythm can take weeks. Sleep will follow if you consistently follow good habits. Once you understand that sleep is a rhythm and you also understand the things that help and hinder sleep, you can make lifestyle changes to help your body clock.[71]

HOW TO EXERCISE WELL

THE EFFECT OF SOCIAL MEDIA ON BODY IMAGE

You don't have to spend long scrolling on social media before being flooded with images of seemingly flawless, perfect bodies. Have you ever looked at these perfect bodies and wished or aspired to look like that? But remember, filters and editing tools are used to create these images and most are *not* real.

> Online editing perpetuates unrealistic standards around fitness and body image, and these standards are nearly impossible to attain without digital help.

It can leave you feeling inadequate when your body doesn't meet these standards of perfection. This can in turn have a detrimental effect on your self-esteem and overall well-being.

Fitness influencers don't just have a powerful influence over how you feel about your body, but also what you *believe* is healthy. While some fitness influencers provide a source of useful information, others promote unrealistic standards, diets and exercise regimes. For example, influencers can highlight body-transformation stories which are often doctored or fake. These stories don't reflect a realistic, healthy or sustainable fitness journey. They can feed you the lie that you can have perfect results if you just follow their advice. You can think that achieving these results is easily attainable. In fact, it's almost impossible and sometimes potentially dangerous. As you scroll, be mindful that influencers are paid to promote their practices like excessive exercise, or the use of supplements or weight-loss products.

Social media is fundamentally focused on *image*; it is and can only ever be two-dimensional. It will *always* prioritise physical appearance over mental health and well-being. The unrealistic standards it sets are often manufactured to make individual social media users popular (and rich), and these standards aren't a true reflection of health, fitness or beauty. In the midst of social media, it's essential to prioritise your well-being and focus on realistic body image and sustainable fitness goals.

MUSCLE OBSESSION

There is a growing trend that has shifted the value from what you do to how you look. With this shift comes a growing pressure to obtain physical perfection. Muscle dysmorphia is a medical condition in which individuals experience persistent dissatisfaction and obsession with their muscles, believing that they are too small, skinny or underdeveloped despite being of normal physique or often very well-built. Signs of muscle dysmorphia may include compulsive exercise, following a very rigid high-protein diet, excessive use of dietary supplements and the use of anabolic steroids. Studies have shown that symptoms of muscle obsession are associated with increased screen time. Specifically among young men, greater time texting and on social media corresponds with more severe symptoms. [72] This points to the growing evidence that watching and comparing yourself to influencers online may lead to feelings of inadequacy, which can be detrimental to men's body image.

THE TECHNIFICATION OF EXERCISE

Targets in exercise have always been with us, whether they involve measuring miles run, time spent cycling, lengths swum or star jumps jumped! We've all become accustomed to these targets, as they play a crucial role in motivating us and keeping us accountable. New Year's resolutions are often centred around exercise routines and fitness aspirations.

Nevertheless, the invention of fitness-tracking technology, whether on our smartphones, smartwatches or personalised fitness devices, has begun a new age of measurability, with the potential for an obsession with the stats. Gone are the days when we mentally checked off our workouts or counted our laps in the pool. Now, we possess a digital record of our activity, which instead of encouraging us often serves as a reminder of our shortcomings. Our fitness facts have become part of our permanent digital footprint, and if we share our stats via an app, they're also available for others to see.

However, don't forget that fitness apps and devices use the same technology as social media to keep us hooked, albeit in the clever guise of promoting our health and well-being. They motivate us with streaks, remind us with push notifications and reward us with an addictive dopamine hit for checking in. While we're focused on tracking our progress, our minds stay invisibly tethered to the technology.

Fitness tracking, too, can transform into an addiction where counting and checking supersedes the intended benefits of exercise. While fixating on these numbers, you may inadvertently lose sight of the fundamental purpose of exercise. Keep asking yourself: Did you enjoy your workout? Did it make you feel better, both mentally and physically? Did it contribute to your overall sense of fitness and well-being?

AM I EXERCISING TOO MUCH?

Ask yourself these questions:

- Do you genuinely enjoy the exercise you're engaging in?
- Do you exercise due to compulsion? Exercise shouldn't only be about physical health but also mental and emotional well-being. It should leave you feeling energised and mentally refreshed, rather than exhausted or stressed.
- Do you exercise and go to the gym obsessively to achieve a certain 'look', especially one you have seen online?
- If you participate in team sports, are these sports a healthy and enjoyable part of your life, or have they become excessively competitive?
- What are your motivations for exercising? Are you doing it for yourself, to stay healthy and to achieve personal goals? Or do you feel pressured by external factors, such as expectations from parents, a desire to look perfect or the need to please a fitness app?

If you have answered 'yes' to several of these questions, or identified with some of the issues in the subsections above, it may be an indication that you have an unhealthy relationship with exercise and your body image. This is nothing to be ashamed of, but now that you have recognised it, take the time to share how you're feeling with a trusted adult, reach out to a mental health charity or seek help from your GP. This is especially important if you're using anabolic steroids, as these can have dangerous medical side effects.

WHAT IF I DON'T EXERCISE ENOUGH?

Being active can make a massive difference to your overall well-being. Exercise releases oxytocin, one of the happy hormones, which will (as it says on the tin) make you feel happier. It also strengthens your muscles, lowers your blood pressure and increases your life expectancy. Exercise, by default, means you're having a break from screens, work or revision. It gives your mind a much-needed break, as few people can exercise while working! Ironically, when you're busiest, you may skip exercise to make time for more work. However, at these pinch moments, exercising will help you cope better with your busyness. Imagine if you were never too busy to take 30 minutes out of your schedule for a quick run or a brisk walk. Exercise will break your stress cycle, making you feel more awake and sharpening your senses. Plus, training is often social, especially in team sports, which helps you connect with peers and create much-needed community. Evidence shows that adolescents who exercise three times a week have higher self-esteem than those who don't exercise at all. [73]

Aside from your physical appearance, I'm sure, like me, you want to feel more alive, active, healthy and happy. However, none of these things happen by chance. Much of our health is determined by our environment, not our genes. You can make change happen. Inside you is enough willpower, strength and self-love to make choices that put your well-being first. You don't have to get it right every day. Your motivation will go up and down. The key is to not give up. Keep going. Make exercise part of your life, and you won't look back. I started running around the school playing fields when I was in sixth form to de-stress before exams. I've been running ever since and this is now a vital part of my well-being. I even met my husband while training for a charity half-marathon.

Think about what kind of exercise makes you feel the best and fits with your values and schedule. My middle daughter hates team sports but loves swimming. In the water she feels free, so we've focused on what makes her feel good. For someone else, the benefits of a team sport can be exponential. You don't have to play at a high level; try to find a local club that's non-selective or takes beginners. Don't be put off if everyone else seems fantastic - all you need to do is start somewhere and your hard work will pay off.

HOW TO GET STARTED

If you've never exercised and don't know where to begin, think about what you enjoy doing, or imagine what you'd like to be able to do. Maybe set yourself a growth challenge or use a logic tree (see page 108 to remind yourself about these) to help you get started. It might seem daunting to start a sport or activity, but it will seem more manageable once you break it down into small steps. Usually, the final task on a logic tree is checking a website or sending an email – a manageable task for most of us. If you follow the steps logically, you'll hopefully find yourself at an exercise class or running meet in the future!

Don't be daunted by the size of the task or how unfit you are. Break your goal into small steps and begin to be more active. The Couch to 5K app is fantastic; it guides you through small incremental steps over nine weeks to take you from walking to running five kilometres! There can be mental and physical hurdles to overcome, but I guarantee you'll feel better once you start some physical activity. Here's a message from the sports coach Joe Wicks on @allontheboard:

> *When you're feeling down or struggling mentally, that's really the time to get physical. Move your body, get outside, elevate your heart rate, push yourself out of your comfort zone. By changing your physical state you will change your mindset. You will feel less stressed, more energised, calmer, more focussed and optimistic. One thing is certain in life... you will always feel better after exercise.* [74]

SOME ACHIEVABLE FITNESS GOALS:

- Aim to walk as much as possible.
- Try the Couch to 5K app (you can repeat weeks if it gets too difficult too quickly).
- Try some free YouTube exercise videos from your home.
- Think about cycling instead of using the car or bus.
- If you use the car or bus, get out/off early and walk the final part of your journey.
- Use the stairs instead of the lift.
- Borrow a dog and go for a walk. (Check out the website www.borrowmydoggy.com.)
- Play frisbee.
- Do 30-star jumps.
- Run down a hill (or up if you're feeling brave).
- Try a water sport - for example, water polo, surfing or paddle boarding.

HOW TO EAT WELL

THE SIGNIFICANCE OF YOUR RELATIONSHIP WITH FOOD

Approaching the issue of food and diet can be a delicate matter. Discussing what you eat and your body image can be associated with fear and loaded with emotion. Many people have a complicated relationship with food. How and what you eat (or don't eat) may reflect how you feel about yourself. Some people overeat to block out difficult emotions. Others may withhold food and lose weight, possibly in an unhealthy way. In extreme circumstances, people may need help to recover from an eating disorder.

I'm not going to share a long list of dos and don'ts or advice on a specific diet. I simply want to help you see that what you eat should be a positive expression of how you feel about yourself. When we love and care for ourselves, we're more likely to eat nourishing and healthy food. We all slip up, and these moments of indulgence are part of everyday life, so please don't be hard on yourself if you don't eat 'perfectly' all the time.

Think about your relationship with food and your physical body. Carefully look at your overall eating patterns and style. Is what you eat, and how, affecting your body image and your self-esteem?

OVEREATING

Some people eat to try to feel better about themselves, while others eat to cope with pain (as a form of self-medicating). However, this behaviour is detrimental to both physical and mental well-being. Overeating can create a vicious cycle that is hard (but not impossible) to break free from. The long-term result of using food to mask pain is almost always obesity, which unfortunately leads to many health complications such as diabetes and heart and joint problems, to name but a few. Losing weight and eating well is a way to love yourself; however, it takes motivation and self-control. As you love and accept yourself more, your ability to look after yourself will grow. At every meal or snack time think, *'What is the most loving action for me in this moment?'* Sometimes it will be to eat the chocolate cake offered to you, but other times it will be to make a healthier choice.

UNDEREATING AND OVER-EXERCISING

Some people spend their entire lives controlling every morsel they eat, never able to enjoy food for fear it will make them fat. You can *try* to fix your feelings about yourself (low self-worth, low self-acceptance or self-loathing) by improving your body. You can *try* to make yourself perfect through gruelling exercise routines and restricted eating rituals. Although it may seem healthy (and be praised) on the outside, it can be very unhealthy on the inside. Having the perfect, Insta-ready body won't solve how you ***feel*** about yourself. Even if you reach your weight and fitness goals, it won't make you like yourself more, unless you change how you feel about yourself on the inside.

THE IMPACT OF SOCIAL MEDIA ON DIET CULTURE

The impact of social media on the food and diet industry is undeniable. The transition online (and the fact that anyone with a following can now be an 'expert') has transformed our access to information and our exposure to intimate details of other people's eating and dietary habits. Fad diets, detoxes, clean eating and extreme weight-loss methods are promoted as normal and healthy, but often with no scientific evidence or proven track record.

The term 'orthorexia' has been coined to describe an emerging obsession with clean eating. It's the belief that food is either 'clean' or 'unclean', 'good' or 'bad'. Orthorexia can result in an extremely restrictive diet that, while apparently healthy and applauded online, is nutritionally deficient and excessively controlling. It's perhaps little more than a socially acceptable form of anorexia that can partially be attributed to the glamorisation of diet culture online. Followers of clean eating can feel intense guilt and shame over eating 'bad' foods and adhere to a level of strict dietary control that's inherently unhealthy (both mentally and physically).

Instead, approach online diet advice and content with a critical mindset. Prioritise evidence-based research or people with a medical background or backing (although even the most respectable healthcare professional may be endorsed to promote a product, so be careful). Try to find a community and online feed that's body positive and makes you feel better about yourself. If you're feeling pressured, anxious or inadequate due to the content, and subsequently the food you consume, consider unfollowing these accounts.

The key is your relationship with yourself - your self-acceptance and self-esteem. As this is healed and restored, your relationship with food and your body image will improve. Turn the focus back onto liking yourself and accepting yourself as you are now. Eating well will follow, because you'll believe you're worth it.

Table 15: Signs that you may be over- or undereating

SIGNS THAT YOU MAY BE UNDEREATING	SIGNS THAT YOU MAY BE OVEREATING
You withhold food to punish yourself.	You regularly binge or overeat; this is linked to feelings of shame and guilt.
You withhold food as a form of control.	You use sugar as a quick fix for low energy.
You have certain foods which are off-limits. You see eating them as *bad*.	You find it hard to stop eating when you start.
You restrict your diet to *clean* food only.	You eat lots of fast food or ready meals.
You judge people's eating habits and think yours are better.	You feel judged by others about what you eat
You feel overweight but are in fact underweight. (A healthy BMI is 18–24. Check your height and weight and calculate your BMI. Base this answer on the facts, not just how you feel.)	You're overweight. (Again, calculate your BMI. Is it over 24?)
You've lost a lot of weight recently.	You've gained a lot of weight and struggle to control your weight.
You're afraid of eating or being forced to eat.	You're afraid of not eating or having to restrict your diet.

TOP TIPS ON HEALTHY EATING:

- Aim to eat three meals a day with healthy snacks in between.
- Try to eat a rainbow of fruit and vegetables every day. This means eating a variety of different-coloured fruit and vegetables.
- Make healthy substitutions when you're hungry, such as a banana instead of a bag of crisps.
- Don't cut out whole food groups unless you have a medically proven allergy or specific reason like you're a vegetarian. Please don't think of any food as *banned* or *bad*.
- If you're overweight, aim to stop eating when you feel 80% full rather than completely full.
- Avoid snacking late at night.
- Drink plenty of water every day.

If you have a complex relationship with food and body image, no book can truly heal this - so please also seek professional help. If this chapter has highlighted issues for you, I would really recommend telling a trusted adult, seeking advice from mental health charities and booking an appointment to see your GP.

CHAPTER 11

THE IMPACT OF SCREEN TIME ON YOUR HEALTH

Faisal was a 19-year-old psychology student. He came to see me asking to be referred to the ADHD clinic. It was the end of his first year at university and he was on the cusp of failing his degree. He was desperate for a diagnosis as it might help him scrape through his finals. I asked Faisal a few questions about what he was struggling with. He told me he couldn't get up in the morning and would then spend the rest of the day trying to write essays but couldn't get anything done as he couldn't concentrate. Faisal said his sleep was poor and he was up most of the night. The cycle then started again the next day, with him being tired and unable to concentrate.

Initially, Faisal's story sounded plausible for ADHD, but I wanted to explore further why Faisal couldn't sleep or concentrate (as the two are closely linked). It became apparent that Faisal slept with his phone on his pillow and spent a lot of the night on social media. Because Faisal felt so awful in the morning, he would lie in bed checking his feeds, as this was the easiest thing to do and required the least effort. Eventually, he would make it to the library and try to write his essays, which were overdue. His phone would sit on the desk next to him. Faisal admitted to checking his phone at least every minute and responding to messages as and when they came. He was left frustrated and anxious as he couldn't focus on writing his essays.

Faisal was convinced this was because he had ADHD, and he was even a little annoyed with me when I suggested that he might have a tech addiction, not ADHD, which was contributing to his poor sleep and difficulty concentrating. I advised a screen detox to see if his concentration improved, and agreed that if he still felt the same without his phone, then I would refer him. I gave Faisal help and advice on how to reduce his screen time, and some apps to help him. Although it was really difficult at first, Faisal did manage to reduce his screen time dramatically, and correspondingly, bit by bit, his sleep, concentration and essay writing all improved.

THE RELATIONSHIP BETWEEN DOPAMINE, ADDICTION AND TECHNOLOGY

We've reviewed how social media can impact your self-esteem, well-being and happiness. But let's consider the wider consequences of the rapid transition from pen and paper to smartphones, not least addiction and overdependence.

The major contributor to the incredible draw of technology is a chemical in the brain called *dopamine*, a neurotransmitter associated with anticipation, pleasure and reward. Dopamine is released when our brains anticipate something nice is going to happen. For example, when we look at a box of chocolates, dopamine is released as our brains anticipate us eating them and how delicious they'll taste. It's released before the chocolate is even in our mouths, making it even harder to resist (as our brains have already anticipated how wonderful it will taste). In another example, slot machine gambling, dopamine is released just before using a slot machine in *anticipation* of winning. It's not released *when* we win (which is much less likely and would make slot machines less addictive). Our brains anticipate winning and the desire to know the outcome, making us want to play, or encouraging us to keep playing.

Many feel-good activities are associated with dopamine release, enhancing their enjoyment and making us more likely to repeat the activity. Dopamine is the brain's prehistoric signal that an activity is safe, happy and pleasurable. Unfortunately, the brain can be tricked (something app designers have taken advantage of) and it often wrongly encourages us to repeat activities that aren't necessarily beneficial.

Tech companies have manipulated the dopamine-reward pathway by designing platforms and apps that provide a constant stream of *anticipatory cues* such as notifications, *likes*, streaks and messages. This means that when we receive notifications or engage with our phones, these cues create a sense of anticipation, triggering the release of dopamine in our brains. Dopamine reinforces the behaviour and makes us want to check our devices again. As with many addictive behaviours, the more we repeat the cycle, the more dopamine we need to maintain a baseline. Over time, the brain needs more dopamine just to feel normal (something called tolerance). The dopamine-hungry brain creates an intense desire, called a craving, which is designed to prompt us to seek out our next dopamine-fuelled social media scroll. And it's not only our sense of anticipation and need for dopamine that tech companies have capitalised on; they've powerfully combined the dopamine hit with our fundamental need to belong and connect.

Face-to-face relationships are vital for well-being (and that even includes the introverts out there). In a recent survey by the BBC, 59% of young people surveyed said they prefer meeting friends face to face rather than online. Yet young people reported meeting online more frequently (55% online and only 40% face to face). [75] Despite the preference for face-to-face connection, so powerful is the dopamine released through social media that the brain rewards you more for being on social media than for seeking real-life connections. In other words, your dopamine system rewards you more for checking TikTok than for meeting friends at the cinema or going out for a meal!

Unfortunately, as we've seen, our brains haven't quite caught up with the 21st century. Many fun-seeking activities result in the indiscriminate release of dopamine. If our brains had a modern-day upgrade, we would probably change the list of dopamine-releasing activities. So, you can see the problem. In trying to protect us, our brains release cortisol in response to perceived danger. And in trying to reward us, our brains release dopamine to anticipate reward. It's a haphazard and unreliable system that requires us to override it. We can't rely on the brain's neurochemical pathways, as they often get it wrong. These pathways can make us more likely to seek the not-so-good activities (as our brains perceive them as safe and reward us with dopamine) and less likely to do the good ones (as our brains link them to danger and release cortisol).

Do you think it's by chance that tech designers have invented something that's so appealing and addictive? The use of the dopamine-reward pathway isn't accidental. Social media sites have been specifically designed with this addictive inbuilt brain pathway at their core. The brightest brains in Silicon Valley have calculated, researched and tested the best way to make these apps more attractive and addictive.

THE ATTENTION ECONOMY

Although most social media apps are free to download, they have an expensive price tag: your time, attention and well-being. The more you endlessly scroll through feeds, the more social media companies make through advertising revenues. This has been dubbed the *attention economy*. Programmers compete for your attention using artificial-intelligence algorithms to keep you engaged and they want you to spend as much time as possible scrolling and messaging. They're not thinking about what we could or should be doing: our homework, playing sport, walking the dog, meeting friends or even eating our tea. Our engagement makes them money. Never before has our time been of such value to multinational companies; Facebook, Instagram, TikTok and Google are all in a race for our attention. [76]

Face-to-face relationships are vital for well-being.

It's not a coincidence that many people are endlessly scrolling on Insta or checking TikTok at 11 p.m. Our feeds have been carefully designed to grab our time and attention; artificial-intelligence algorithms curate our feeds to align them with our interests. Without realising it, we can fall into their attention-grabbing feeds carefully designed for us and our unique interests. And because of the brain's ability to adapt and grow neural pathways, the more often we repeat the behaviour, the more it becomes hardwired in our brains. Ultimately, no one checks whether these algorithms are pushing material that's suitable and safe for users, especially those under 18. The coroner ruled that social media posts played a significant role in the tragic death of teenager Molly Russell. Sadly, whilst at her lowest ebb, the posts she viewed were full of content on depression and self-harm. [77]

So, what can you do? We've already established that we want, like and need our phones and social media. And I've already promised I won't tell you to stop using them! But somewhere there's a fine line: having a smartphone and enjoying it, but not becoming too dependent. Studies have shown that social media has a dose-dependent relationship with self-esteem - in other words, people who use social media more tend to have lower self-esteem. Conversely, they've shown that when young people spend less than an hour a day on social media, there's no measurable negative impact on their well-being. If you can reduce your time on social media, [78] you can make the extra time you save beneficial to your well-being, whilst also avoiding the negative consequences.

I'm a sensible mother of three who's spent much of the last five years researching and talking about social media addiction. I've had Facebook since my late twenties and would spend ten minutes most days scrolling. As I previously mentioned, I did develop a fixation on the news app at one point, but overall I used my phone with moderation. And then I joined Instagram, and I have to confess I very quickly became a repeat offender! I joined with good intentions. My book idea had been rejected by several agents, and I was advised to increase my presence on social media. So, with some reluctance, I signed up as @thehealthyselfiedr and started posting well-being quotes and carousels. What began with good intentions became an obsession. *Likes* and followers began to hold value for me. I could feel the draw to check and recheck how a post was performing. I could feel the power of the algorithm at work and the draw of my dopamine-sensitive brain to the platform. I now have to have my phone physically out of reach to prevent me from quickly checking for notifications. Leaving my phone out of the bedroom is the only way to ensure it's not the first thing I check in the morning. I can't help but reflect on the power of Instagram if posting a few well-being quotes has had this effect on me.

WHEN DOES A HABIT BECOME AN ADDICTION?

Social media and gaming are such a widely accepted part of our society that many people are on their devices a significant majority of the time. This makes it challenging to recognise if your use has tipped into dependent or addictive behaviour (for example, needing to do that activity more and more and finding it hard to stop), because there'll always be someone who checks their social media or game more than you. This can falsely reassure you that your own use is healthy and within your control. You'll always be able to make a favourable comparison with a fellow user and feel better about your own tech use. However, it's not this other user you need to focus on; it's you.

ASK YOURSELF:

- Is your use of technology harming any areas of your life? Have you lost friends, got lower grades, argued at home or become isolated because of your gaming or social media habits? Do you choose screen time instead of other activities that you used to enjoy?
- Do you find you're mindlessly scrolling or gaming?
- How does your time on social media or gaming make you feel? Do you struggle to like yourself? Do you compare yourself with others, especially after time online? Do you feel worse about yourself and your life after spending time on social media?
- Do you find it hard to stop even though you recognise the downsides? If your answer to more than one of these questions is yes, it's worth thinking about whether you're spending too long online.

These questions are designed to make you think. Addiction is a powerful word and often brings up negative images of drugs, gambling and alcohol. However, we can be addicted to anything from chocolates to exercise. Addictive behaviour describes any behaviour that we can't stop, despite the negative consequences and attempts we make to cut down. A recent study found 16% of those under the age of 30 had signs of smartphone addiction. [79]

Smartphone addiction isn't currently classified as an addiction by the World Health Organization. However, many people, including medical professionals, recognise that we can become dependent on our phones and this dependence can have negative consequences. There are similar behaviours to those seen in other addictions - for example, finding it hard to stop despite the negative impact, and exponentially increasing use over time.

HOW MUCH TIME DO YOU SPEND ON AVERAGE ON YOUR PHONE?

You can find this out by checking your screen time in the settings of your phone.

HOURS SPENT	TOTAL
Per day	
Per week (x 7)	
Per year (x 52)	

Table 16: Signs you may be addicted to your phone

	TICK IF IT APPLIES TO YOU
I sleep with my phone next to me or under my pillow.	
I scroll myself to sleep.	
My phone is the first thing I check in the morning.	
I lie about how much time I spend on my phone.	
My friends and family have expressed concern about the amount of time I spend on my phone.	
I have trouble getting things done at school or home due to the time I spend on my phone.	
I check my phone whilst doing other activities.	
I am constantly distracted by my phone.	
I check my social media accounts repeatedly and become anxious if I'm unable to do so.	
I feel angry or irritable if my phone use is interrupted.	
I have had an accident or injury due to my phone use.	
I have a weak or non-existent in-person social life, but I have lots of friends on social media.	

I feel isolated and struggle to connect with my friends and family.

I reach for my phone in moments of boredom or to alleviate stress.

I have experienced phantom vibration (thinking my phone is buzzing when it's not).

I have trouble limiting phone use and find it hard to stop using it.

Adapted from questions by the Addiction Center. [80]

DISTRACTION

Another enormous impact of the use of technology is its ability to distract us. Without even considering the science, we know that our phones are undoubtedly a constant source of distraction. Not only do they beep and buzz, but they also flash up notifications and reward us (with dopamine, streaks and *likes*) for checking them. They can distract us from completing tasks, interrupt conversations and interfere with our sleep. How often do you check your phone for one reason and end up getting completely distracted by something else? We mean to do one thing and then a notification flashes up, and before we know it, we've lost half an hour (and not completed the original task). Once we start scrolling through our feeds, it's incredibly hard to stop. There are no stopping cues (unlike a book, there's no end of the chapter to remind us to take a break); the feed just goes on and on. Although it's *us* scrolling on our phones, are we actually consciously choosing to do it? How often do we get lost in time and spend much longer than we planned scrolling? Such is the power of scrolling on social media that Dr Steven Hassan, one of the world's foremost experts on mind control, cults and similar destructive organisations, describes it as akin to being unethically hypnotised. [81]

Being distracted by our phones matters because it stops us from focusing on the world around us. It takes time to refocus after being distracted by your phone. It's been found that every time you have a major distraction it takes 23 minutes to recover from the distraction. [82] It's also been shown that when students use social media for more than 100 minutes a day, there's a significant reduction in their school performance. The effect is significantly worse for those using their phones in the classroom. [83] Imagine how much more effectively you could work if you weren't distracted by your phone. Try using an app blocker or deep-focus mode on your phone and see how much more you get done.

CONCENTRATION AND ADHD

Smartphones also appear to be impacting our ability to concentrate. People are spending more and more time on social media, especially on short, attention-grabbing clips (that stimulate excessive amounts of dopamine). As a result, they're finding it harder and harder to concentrate on more meaningful tasks which require more concentration, like reading a book or even watching a film (without scrolling on their phones at the same time). Apart from some phone-free time at school, often there's now rarely a waking (or sleeping) moment when a young person is apart from their phone. The average person checks their phone 150 times a day. [84] These minor phone checks can seem harmless, fun or a welcome break. However, collectively, they can erode concentration, increase anxiety and hardwire the brain to crave the next dopamine hit.

You may think you can multitask (for example, check your phone and write an essay at the same time), but the reality is that despite taking in millions of bits of information, your brain can only focus on one thing at a time. When you multitask, you're in fact switching rapidly back and forth between individual tasks. This means you waste time and energy alternating between tasks instead of focusing on doing one thing well. [85] The practice of multi-screening (using two devices at the same time) is also a form of multitasking, and it can reduce your attention and enjoyment of both tasks. It can also cause mental fatigue, as your brain is constantly switching between devices and trying to take all the information in.

ADHD is a neuro-diverse condition which manifests as hyperactivity and attention deficit (difficulty in concentrating). It appears to be dramatically on the rise, especially in young people who are struggling to concentrate in school, university and the workplace. While I have every belief in the reality, complexity and frustrations for ADHD sufferers, I also see a very high overlap of ADHD symptoms and the effects of high technology usage. As we consider the effects of technology on the brain, we need to acknowledge that at least some ADHD symptoms could be caused by distraction and loss of focus due to smartphone use. It's a two-way street: people with ADHD are more likely to have their symptoms worsened by tech use, and others who use tech excessively may develop ADHD-like symptoms as a result.

This phenomenon appears far worse with TikTok. For anyone not familiar with the intensely popular video-sharing app, it allows you to watch an endless scrolling feed of very short, attention-grabbing and often funny clips. Clever algorithms tailor content to your interests to ensure your maximum engagement. There may not seem to be anything different about TikTok, but because the videos are so short (7.5 seconds on average), they're particularly dopamine stimulating and, therefore, addictive. Repeated use literally trains the brain to desire very short, attention-grabbing material (ideally with a large hit of dopamine to go with it). However, the real world, education and the workplace require the opposite qualities: patience, consistency, an ability to stay focused on a task (even when something is difficult or boring) and resilience. Such is the dopamine response and the subsequent addictive qualities of the app that it's been held partially responsible for a decline in concentration in young people. The term *TikTok brain* has been used to describe some of the negative aspects associated with the platform including lower attention spans, reduced working memory, and increased anxiety and depression. [86]

It's quite a scary thought. Frequent social media use changes the grey matter of your brain (the thinking bit of your brain that affects how you respond socially and regulate your emotions). And from the evidence we have so far, this isn't a positive evolution.

There are many, many more people like Faisal (who we met at the beginning of the chapter) out there. Because people are so used to being distracted by their phones, some have completely forgotten what it's like to concentrate! Maybe you're even struggling to read this or do your school work. How many times has your phone bleeped, flashed or vibrated during this chapter alone? Maybe it's worth stopping now and putting it on silent or 'do not disturb' mode and trying to read this chapter again. Is it easier to read? Does it make more sense? Think what a difference it could make to your schoolwork and exam scores if the time you spent working was more effective and efficient. There's nothing worse than putting the time in but not getting the results you want. Your time is precious. Choose to make it as effective as possible by reclaiming your concentration and putting down your phone (even if it's just for a short period of time).

PHYSICAL HEALTH

Physical health problems associated with increased mobile phone use include insomnia, reduced fitness, unhealthy eating habits and obesity, headaches, neck pain and repetitive strain injury. Studies have shown that the blue light emitted by phones stops us from sleeping and that excessive use can be associated with headaches and migraines. [87]

PSYCHOLOGICAL HEALTH

There's been a rapid rise in mental health problems among young people. You may have read about it in the news, talked about it at school or university, or know someone close to you who's struggling. You may even be struggling yourself. If so, you're not alone and it's really important that you know it's not your fault. In 2016, one in nine children had a diagnosed mental health problem. This had risen quickly to one in six in 2021 (undoubtedly, some of this was because of the pandemic, but even prior to this it had risen sharply). At 14, when young people reported their own symptoms, 24% of girls and 9% of boys were identified as suffering with depression. [88]

UNDERSTANDING ANXIETY AND DEPRESSION

Anxiety is a fear-based disorder. People with anxiety experience repetitive worrying thoughts, often accompanied by physical symptoms such as a racing heart, sweaty palms and rapid breathing. You can experience just the physical or the emotional symptoms. Anxiety can be linked to several things or events (for example, health, social activities or exams). It's normal to worry, but what distinguishes it as a disorder is the *excessive* worry; it's when worry gets out of control that it can become problematic. Many people think and worry about things that are in the future (everyone does it). However, if your anxiety is stopping you from doing things and is having a negative impact on your life, then it's worth addressing the issue. You can start by talking to your parents, teachers or GP.

Depression describes a feeling of persistent low mood and a loss of interest in things that you used to enjoy. Anxiety is such an unpleasant experience that it can lower your mood and it often goes hand in hand with depression. The spiral of negative and anxious thoughts can make you feel depressed, as it stops you from doing the things that make you feel better - for example, social anxiety can stop you from meeting friends socially or exercising.

Low mood (or depression) can be a response to really difficult things that might have happened in your life. Losing someone you love, your parents splitting up or experiencing abuse (along with a multitude of other very difficult things that can happen in the world) are really difficult things to have experienced or be going through. It's natural to feel sad as a response to difficult life events, and no one can feel happy all the time (especially when they're going through something tough). The key is getting the right support so that you can gradually walk through the trauma and begin to heal and recover. Often the support needed may be from a health professional or counsellor. Don't try to go it alone or suffer in silence. It can be difficult asking for help, but it's worth it. We can't avoid life trauma, but we can - however long it takes - survive it and come out the other side.

Similarly, many people with depression may not have experienced a specific trauma. We've talked about how your use of social media could be impacting how you feel about yourself, which can contribute to mental health issues. This doesn't make how you're feeling any less important or valid, and it's still definitely not your fault. Likewise, you need to ask for help from school, your parents, mental health charities and/or your GP.

MENTAL HEALTH AND THE IMPACT OF SOCIAL MEDIA

Remember that although we don't fully understand why, there appears to be an increased vulnerability in heavy social media users to mental illness. I'm not blaming social media for how you're feeling, but it almost certainly isn't helping. We've looked at the fact it can lower your self-esteem and your ability to like and accept yourself. It can also interfere with your sleep and physical activity (both of which are essential for your well-being). All these things can have a major impact on how you feel and your mood. You won't suddenly feel different when you use social media, but it can, bit by bit, change the way you feel about yourself and your life. By the age of 19, heavy social media users have been shown to be less happy with their lives, with lower life satisfaction, than users who spend less than an hour a day on it. [89] If you want to feel better, there are lots of things that you can do. Remember, you can control how much time you spend online and the content you view.

THE IMPACT OF LOCKDOWN

Josh was in Year 6 when the pandemic hit. He missed school camp and the end-of-year play, and all he got was a leavers' hoodie in the post. After all those years at primary school looking forward to his final summer term, he missed out on everything. He already found schoolwork difficult and refused to take part in online school during the first lockdown. Instead, he gamed with his friends, playing Fortnite. He didn't go out much and stayed in his PJs all day. At first it was fun, like a giant holiday. But then he stopped being able to sleep and worried about even going outside for a walk. The place he felt safe and fulfilled was in his room, gaming. Being good at gaming made him feel better about himself. Gradually, he gamed more and more.

By the time he was due to start Year 7, Josh was finding it hard to leave his room. He started Year 7 at a local secondary school, but he found it overwhelming. After a few weeks, Josh complained about headaches and spent more and more time staying at home. He hated school and by the end of his first term simply refused to go in. Josh continued to game, and his mood deteriorated while his anxiety increased. He stopped washing and often slept in his clothes. One day, aged 13, he confided in his mum that he was feeling suicidal. This triggered a referral to CAMHS (Child and Adolescent Mental Health Service) and Hospital Education (a special home-based school system for those who can't manage school for a period of time).

Josh is now attending Hospital Education and, bit by bit, his mood is improving. He now gets up every day and his gaming is under better control. He still has a long way to go, but he's making steady progress in the right direction.

Technology became even more important during the pandemic. Trapped at home on our own, screen-time limits were thrown out the window and our dependence on technology increased dramatically. Screens became our online classrooms and offices, and with the playground taken away, social media and gaming became the primary source of socialisation and entertainment for young people. We didn't just suffer from stress, anxiety and loss from the pandemic itself - we also experienced the absence of many positives in our lives, such as face-to-face communication, traditional work and school routines, and socialising opportunities.

It seems that young people, like you, were hit the hardest by the pandemic. In 2017, only 10% of 17- to 19-year-olds were dealing with possible mental health issues. But by 2022, that number had shot up to 25% for people in this same age group.[90] This group were between 14 and 16 years old in 2020, and you may well be part of the group. You missed out on vital learning in school, faced online learning instead, and experienced the cancellation of GCSEs and A levels. These were tough times and you had to face them mostly on your own.

Many young people have bounced back after the pandemic and returned to normal life and screen normality (whatever that may be). However, for a small minority there's been a lasting and ongoing impact. Despite the world moving on and restrictions ending, a minority are still trapped at home. School attendance remains much lower than before the pandemic. There are complex reasons for this, but underlying gaming disorders and an increase in mental health problems are possible reasons.[91]

There are thousands of similar stories across the UK and beyond, where lockdown has triggered a mental health crisis in young people. Many are still in crisis and haven't made it back to school. If this relates to you, I really encourage you to get some help and tell someone how you're feeling. A good starting point is your GP; you can even fill in an online request for advice at most surgeries.

GAMING

Lara's parents were worried and had contacted the GP surgery several times. They reported that she was refusing to eat and was losing weight. They were afraid she had an eating disorder. Lara was refusing to go to school and was spending hours a day in her bedroom. Previous attempts to engage with her had achieved no actual progress, and she'd been referred to the eating disorders team.

When I met Lara, I wanted to understand why she wasn't eating. At first, she complained her mother didn't cook for her. I wondered if there was a significant neglect issue (where parents don't provide the appropriate care for their children). However, on deeper probing, Lara confessed that her mother brought food to her bedroom, but she was too busy gaming to stop and eat. The true story then unravelled. Lara had gamed more during the first lockdown. As time passed, she lost control of her gaming. Lara lost interest in friends and other hobbies and would game in preference to everything else, even eating. She was now refusing to go to school as she was too tired and anxious to get up in the mornings after a night spent gaming. She rarely left her room and had even wet herself on several occasions, as she didn't want to stop to go to the bathroom. Gaming left her anxious and feeling low. She didn't feel safe leaving her room and this perpetuated the cycle. Her world had shrunk to a virtual one.

There's an even more impactful story surrounding gaming, as unlike heavy social media use, the World Health Organization *has* recognised gaming disorder as an addiction. This means it's a defined and diagnosable illness. Gaming disorder is defined as a pattern of behaviour characterised by the following three criteria:

- Finding it hard to stop
- Prioritising gaming to the extent that gaming takes precedence over other interests and daily activities
- Continuation or escalation of time gaming despite the occurrence of negative consequences

Gaming disorder doesn't just mean spending a lot of time on your console and finding it hard to stop (as that's the very nature of gaming and would mean most gamers have it). To diagnose gaming disorder, the behaviour pattern must be of sufficient severity to result in significant problems in the personal, family, social, educational or other important areas of your life. It also needs to have been a problem for at least 12 months, so a binge over the Christmas holidays doesn't count.[92]

To put this in context, 90% of 13- to 18-year-olds in the UK game online.[93] Most game safely within normal limits. However, the World Health Organization estimates that approximately 2% of gamers have an addiction problem.[94] Based on nearly 7,000 participants, recent research from Oxford University suggests that more than 1.5 million people in the UK suffer from gaming disorder.[95]

THE POWER BEHIND GAMING

ADDICTION AND DOPAMINE

Gaming has been designed to be highly addictive in three main ways: physiological (body), psychological (mind) and social (connections and friendships). Game designers use every trick in the book to make their games more and more interactive, realistic and addictive. They make reaching the next level only *just* accessible. They make you feel like you're making progress and doing well.[96] Like smartphones, gaming releases vast quantities of dopamine, causing the player to feel good and making the experience more addictive. Gaming is an immersive experience. Games are so realistic and all-absorbing that you can almost live in and through the game. Gaming also fulfils two very important domains:

- **Social and emotional:** Gaming superficially meets emotional and social needs to the extent it can replace the real world. Game designers have made it highly social, creating a way for you to connect and develop a sense of belonging. The team element brings purpose and creates a community, meaning gamers don't want to leave a game and let their team down. Combining all these elements in one easy place can make it highly addictive.
- **Reward and purpose:** Game designers understand how often to reward players, how to tailor their games to specific age groups and genders, and how, in the process, to extract as much money as possible. The virtual gaming world can also be a much easier place to inhabit than the real world with its complicated relationships, conflicts and slow reward-to-achievement ratio.

The combination of these factors works powerfully to create a tight draw to gaming. School refusal is often the point at which gaming disorder is diagnosed. It's a critical point on the gaming disorder trajectory that can no longer be ignored by teachers or parents. There are many reasons a gamer may refuse to go to school. They may be too tired to get up in the morning having gamed late into the night. Or they may be so psychologically attached to their gaming console and the distraction and comfort it brings that they don't want to leave the house. Or there may be a complex myriad of mental health issues (often social anxiety, low self-esteem and depression) that trap a young person in their bedroom. The real world of education is complex and fraught with pressure and failures, so the virtual world of gaming can be a safer place for a young person to inhabit. Cam Adair, a previous gaming addict and founder of Game Quitters, says:

You begin to live in a world where you expect instant gratification. Games are so immersive that it's easy to play for hours and hours without even noticing that a minute has gone by. They allow you to escape and see measurable progress. They are social and create an environment where you feel safe and in control.[97]

TIME TO CRAVE?

The *Cambridge Dictionary* defines a craving as *'a powerful desire for something or a strong wanting of what promises enjoyment or pleasure'.*[98] Ultimately, cravings are a natural symptom of the need for a particular activity or substance. Cravings can be physical (for example, the body's reaction to nicotine, drug or alcohol withdrawal) or psychological (for example, behavioural actions that make you do a specific activity). In technology dependence, the cravings aren't physical; nothing physically unpleasant will happen if you don't check your phone or game. However, you may experience a strong psychological desire (a craving) to check your favourite technology. Physical cravings associated with substance addiction can last for five to ten minutes. However, the psychological urge to check your phone may only last ten to twenty seconds. It's often a momentary impulse. Still, people often respond to these cravings and check their technology without even thinking. This strengthens the dopamine response cycle in the brain and will subsequently increase future cravings.

The best advice is to deal with cravings as they come, one by one. This requires you to recognise and interrupt your thought pattern when the cravings hit. Try stopping what you're doing and doing something entirely different for a few moments. Or try turning your phone over, face down, and ignoring it. You can redirect your focus from the craving and thereby overcome it. You don't *need* to respond to the urge and you can choose not to. You'll find that the desire will pass quickly, and each time you ignore a craving, you weaken the dopamine feedback loop in your brain and it will be easier to resist the craving next time.

TOP TIPS FOR MANAGING CRAVINGS:

- Remind yourself that the craving will pass.
- Remember that nothing terrible will happen if you don't check your phone.
- Put your phone out of sight or turn it face down.
- Try to distract yourself.
- Think, why am I checking my phone? Do I need to? Is there something better I can do with my time?
- Reward yourself each time you don't check your phone.

The best advice is to deal with cravings as they come, one by one.

EXERCISES TO HELP REDUCE YOUR SCREEN TIME

TIME FOR CHANGE

Consider what you'd like to change about your screen and social media use. Imagine how you'd like your tech use to be in six months or one year from now. Imagine how you'd like to feel about yourself when you scroll on social media. A recent study found that reducing screen time to sixty minutes a day for four weeks improved perceptions of body image in young adults. [99] Everyone will have different goals because technology impacts each of us differently. Although a few people do choose to give up completely, for most people, it's about finding a way to reduce screen time. What's important is to identify an area in which you'd like to change or grow.

- How would you like to change your screen time?
- How much would you like to reduce your screen time by per day?
- How many times an hour would you, ideally, like to check your phone?
- Would you like to have your phone off or on downtime for significant periods of time?
- Would you like to leave your phone out of your bedroom at night?
- Would you like to post less on social media?
- Would you still like to use your social media but make it safer and less addictive?

Hopefully, you've recognised an area you'd like to change, and this is the moment to take back control. Don't allow your phone to control you, but be smart and learn how to control it. There are different stages to changing behaviour, especially something so engrained as checking your phone.

STAGES OF CHANGE

1. PREPARE

The first step is to be prepared. Read the ideas at the end of this chapter and think about which method would be most effective for you. Make a plan. Prepare for change. You can do this by deleting apps or setting time limits. Ideally, tell other people your plan or try to cut back with someone else. Changing habits is so much easier if you do it with your friends or family.

2. ACTION

Once you're ready, set a date and begin your screen reduction or behavioural changes. As you can see from the list on page 200, there are lots of different things you can try. Don't be despondent if you find it difficult; keep going. If one method isn't working, try something else. There'll be some days when you feel more motivated than others. If you have a bad day and use your screen loads, don't worry! The important thing is not to give up. Be kind to yourself and try again the next day. Changing the relationship with your screen will take time, and that's okay! There's no hurry. The main aim is to eventually achieve the goal you've set for yourself.

3. MAINTAIN

Once you've established a new rhythm, you're ready for the maintenance phase. This means keeping up the good habits. It's not the time to stop making any effort, as you can easily slip back into old habits. The maintenance phase is a bit like walking on a treadmill: you just need to keep going! Again, you'll have good days and bad ones. The main thing is to maintain the progress you've made. Reflect on how you feel and how far you've come. Hopefully, you'll be finding that you have more time and that you're feeling better about yourself. Don't let go of the positive changes you've made!

Illustration 16: The stages of change

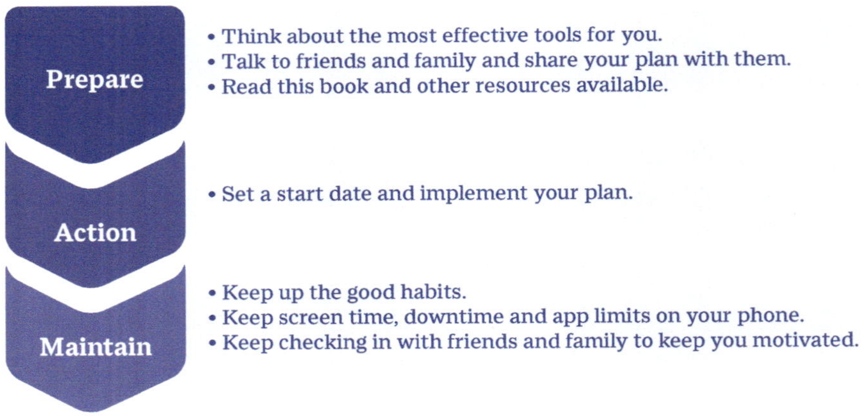

HOW TO REDUCE YOUR SCREEN TIME

1. SET YOUR TIME LIMITS

Both newer iPhones and androids have built-in programs to help you check your screen time and set limits. You may also have this feature as part of parental control software on your device(s). Setting screen-time limits can be helpful. It's a great way to prevent you from scrolling aimlessly. It also helps you ration your phone use, as you don't want your screen time to run out before the end of the day.

First, consider your current usage; you can find this out in screen-time reports. Then think about what a realistic screen-time allowance would be for you. For example, if you're currently using your phone for four hours a day, consider cutting down to two hours a day (gaining a whopping fourteen hours a week of extra time). I'd recommend only one to two hours a day and ideally less than one hour on social media. Don't do it all at once; instead, make a plan to cut back each week incrementally. You can write yourself a screen-saver reminder like *'Do you need to check me?'*. Or use an app like the Forest app to encourage you not to check your phone (see page 204 for more information). Aim to cut your usage over eight weeks by twenty minutes a week so that you gradually learn to be more efficient with your screen time and check your phone less. If you cut back slowly, you're less likely to get psychological withdrawal symptoms.

As you cut back, you'll need something to fill the extra time. Use the spare time for something positive: going on a run, drawing a picture, cooking a treat, reading a book or even watching an episode on Netflix. Replacing screen time with something else helps keep you motivated, as you can see the positive gain of using the time for something else. With each positive step forward you make, reward yourself. Once your screen usage is down, keep the time limits on to reduce your chance of a relapse. Reflect on how you feel and remind yourself that life is better when you're not so attached to your phone.

SUMMARY OF THE STEPS TO REDUCE YOUR SCREEN TIME:

- Calculate your current usage.
- Decide what your ideal usage would be.
- Create a plan to reduce your screen time over eight weeks.
- Choose a positive replacement activity.
- Set the screen-time limits on your phone.
- Reward yourself for each incremental reduction you make in your phone usage.
- Invite friends and family to join you in reducing their screen time. It's always easier to make a change with friends and family doing the same thing to support you.

2. TURN OFF YOUR NOTIFICATIONS

Notifications tell us if we have new messages in a particular app. They say to our brains, *'This is urgent. Check me now. You may miss out. It can't wait. Go on, check me.'* They're designed to distract us and get our attention. However, turning off notifications for apps and emails is very simple. It instantly reduces your phone's ability to distract you and puts you back in control. You can then check your apps when you want to.

My husband was part of a work management WhatsApp group with poor time boundaries. It would frustrate him to find multiple late-night WhatsApp messages to which he felt he had to respond. After a few weeks of growing WhatsApp tension, I turned off his notifications. He could then choose to check the group during work hours but was blissfully unaware of all the late-night messaging.

Turning off notifications puts you back in control. Try turning all of your notifications off. You can then choose when and how often you'll check your social media feeds and emails. There's very little that can't wait for a few hours, and if something is more urgent, then in my experience the person will get hold of you somehow!

3. USE THE 'DO NOT DISTURB' MODE OR FOCUS MODE

You can enable the 'do not disturb' mode on your phone to silence incoming calls and messages while you're trying to focus on a specific task. You can still allow particular numbers (for example, your parents or people in your favourites list), so you won't be entirely uncontactable. This can be especially helpful when you're trying to study, as it reduces the temptation to check your phone and enables you to focus. You can use this mode for prolonged periods or just an hour to help you to concentrate.

4. SET DOWNTIME

You can set your phone to go automatically into 'do not disturb' mode at specific times. The screen will darken, and you will not be alerted by messages, phone calls or notifications. It's a good compromise if you don't feel comfortable or able to leave your phone outside of your bedroom at night.

Setting downtime overnight can help you get a better night's sleep and it detaches you from your phone for a few hours. There's very little that can't really wait until the morning. You may feel you're missing out on the chat overnight, but it's a good idea to try to balance this with your need for sleep. Ask yourself: are you checking your phone at night because it's the best thing for you? Or, is it because you feel you should and you're worried about missing out? Maybe you could get up a little earlier, so you've got time to check your feeds before school. Could you try to tackle this as a friendship group? It's unlikely that it's just you struggling to sleep if everyone in your group is messaging overnight.

5. CONSIDER LEAVING YOUR PHONE OUTSIDE OF YOUR BEDROOM AT NIGHT

If you've mastered downtime overnight, the next step is to not have your phone with you at all! Experts agree that using smart technology within an hour of bedtime can disrupt your sleep.[100] I know this sounds difficult, but remember, liking and caring for yourself means making a few tough choices now so you'll feel better later. My telling you it will be better for you in the future may not massively motivate you. But can you trust me on this one? Suppose you try having your phone out of your room and see how you feel. You can do this in small, incremental steps and do things that will make it easier, such as buying an alarm clock so that you don't need to use the alarm on your phone.

HOW TO WEAN YOURSELF OFF HAVING YOUR PHONE IN YOUR BEDROOM:

1. Put it on silent or downtime overnight.
2. If your phone is under your pillow, move it to beside your bed.
3. Move it further away from your bed, so that you can't reach it without getting up.
4. Try putting it by the door, and then on the other side of the door.
5. Finally, leave it in a different room all night.

This one change will probably be the most significant thing you can do to impact your life positively. If you can detach yourself from your phone at night, you'll sleep better. And if you sleep better, everything else in your life will, to a certain extent, improve too.

6. TRY A FLIP COVER

Using a flip cover serves two important functions: first, it protects your screen and prevents breakages, and second, your phone becomes less tempting and attractive. Rather than seeing your screen saver flash up with every message or notification, you only see the flip-case cover!

7. GREYSCALE YOUR PHONE

Greyscaling your phone makes the screen black and white. With greyscale set, you're less likely to check and spend time on the phone as it's less appealing. It's like looking at a half-eaten doughnut instead of a triple chocolate fudge cake. The stale doughnut is less tempting, although you might still eat it anyway!

8. HIDE APPS

Removing apps from sight makes you less likely to use and check them. Again, it's like hiding the chocolates in the cupboard. They're still there, but you're less likely to eat them because you can't see them. To make apps less appealing, you can move them from your home screen or put them in a folder. To remove temptation completely, you can delete the app altogether.

9. TRY THE FOREST APP

This handy little app rewards you for not checking your phone. When you use the app, you turn on the timer for a designated period - for example, one hour, while writing an essay. Whilst the timer is on, your screensaver becomes a handy reminder not to check your phone, as it has prompts like *'don't look at me'*. If you complete the designated time period without checking your phone, you earn tokens as a reward and these tokens go towards planting real trees. And you might do better in your homework or essay writing too! [1]

10. ENJOY SCREEN-FREE TIME

Having screen-free time allows our brains to rest and unwind. It breaks the cortisol stress cycle and gives us those all-important micro-breaks. A regular screen-free period is like a reset period; it helps uncouple our brains from excessive technology use. It breaks the cycle of technology dependence, as we prove to ourselves that we can (even if only for a brief period) live without our phones. This empowers us to make more balanced choices throughout the rest of the week.

HOW TO DETOX FROM TECH:

- Start by setting specific tech-free times like mealtimes and trips out.
- Next, try implementing a tech-free hour once a week, then gradually extend it to two hours weekly.
- If this goes well, increase to a weekly tech-free half day or even a whole day.
- Try keeping the tech-free time and day the same, so you build it into the rhythm of your week.

CONCLUSION

To conclude, I hope that (contrary to what you might think I would say) you'll continue to use your phone and take selfies. I hope you'll continue to enjoy social media, gaming and connecting with others online. The difference now is that I hope you'll enjoy these online activities with a greater understanding and insight into how they make you think and feel. I hope you'll be able to evaluate your own thoughts and online activity in light of whether or not they're beneficial to you. I really hope that you like yourself more for the wonderful person that you are, and that as a result you're making healthier and wiser choices about how you spend your time and what you believe about yourself.

Life is full of joy, excitement and successes but is also fraught with inevitable frustrations, setbacks and disappointments. As you navigate life, remember that you're not alone. In difficult moments, reach for your friends, not your phone. You don't need to strive to be perfect, but instead I hope that you can accept your imperfections and grow to become your own healthy selfie.

APPENDIX

INTERNET SAFETY

This is a topic that's well covered in schools and colleges. I've compiled a few helpful guides on avoiding some of the most typical dangers online. The guidelines are always the same. Make sure you know who you're talking to online, and always tell a trusted adult if you feel uncomfortable.

HOW TO STAY SAFE ON SOCIAL MEDIA

Social media is fun, distracting, creative and validating. New platforms and features are added almost weekly. What is there not to like? However, we've seen that social media can damage your self-esteem by increasing comparison to others, and that you can become addicted to it. There are also many other concerns related to social media use – for example, cyberbullying, grooming and self-harm algorithms. Few of us today would want to give up social media completely. However, could you consider making some compromises to make your use safer and less addictive? These are some simple ways you can change how you use social media. They're not designed to stop you from using it altogether, but they'll make it safer and less compelling. You don't need to try them all, but consider trying one or two.

1. KEEP YOUR ACCOUNTS PRIVATE

Meta (the parent company of Facebook, Instagram and WhatsApp), after intense international pressure, has recently made changes to their platforms to make them safer for adolescents. New users will now have their accounts set to private by default, and adults will be restricted from messaging teens who don't follow them. However, if you have an existing profile or profile on another platform, it will still be public by default, meaning anyone can view your profile and posts and message you directly. Changing (or keeping) your account to 'private' means that only your friends and contacts can view your profile and message you directly. I'll admit this makes social media less exciting and probably reduces the number of *likes* and followers you'll have. It may sound boring and defeat the point of social media for you. However, this simple change dramatically reduces the ability of a stranger to contact you, protecting you from cyberbullying and online grooming, and in this way, it protects your self-esteem.

2. ADD COMMENT CONTROLS

One of the most damaging aspects of social media is the prevalence of negative comments and cyberbullying. Fortunately, most social media platforms offer tools to help users manage and mitigate these issues. You can use comment controls and filters to reduce the impact of negative comments on your posts. Additionally, many platforms allow you to control who can comment on your posts, block specific individuals or limit comments to your contacts only. By disabling comments for specific posts or all posts, you can protect yourself from the harmful effects of hurtful comments.

You can also turn on advanced comment filtering (it's off by default). These filters work differently on each platform but generally aim to hide inappropriate or disrespectful comments. For instance, on Instagram you can enable the hidden-words setting or create a custom list of words, phrases or emojis that you want to be automatically hidden from your posts. You have the option to hide your own *like* count or choose not to view the *like* count on others' posts. This means you can post without needing the reassurance of a *like* count. It frees you to post because you want to, without worrying about other people's approval!

3. TURN OFF GPS SETTINGS

The most well-known example of GPS tracking is the Snap Map on Snapchat. By default, Snapchat users have their exact location tracked on the Snap Map, and if your profile is public, almost anyone can track your location. Snap Map has implications for your privacy and safety, as anyone can know exactly where you are. You can deactivate the Snap Map by going into settings and turning on 'Ghost Mode'.

Likewise, on Facebook if you have your location data turned on, anyone you're in contact with over the app (even if they're not a friend) can track your exact location. By going into settings, it's easy to turn 'location data' off and disable this feature.

On Instagram, if you have the 'Add to Map' function turned on, the app will geotag the location of where your photos are uploaded. If your profile is public and you upload pictures from your home or school, anybody can see those locations. It's worth checking your account settings and turning this feature off to ensure your location isn't tagged.

CYBERBULLYING

The statistics on cyberbullying are stark: 20% of children experience some form of bullying online, whether via social media, text or online gaming. [101] The long-term impact of cyberbullying can have a lasting effect on your emotional well-being. Bullying at school has always been painful and upsetting, but previously it was limited to the school day. Cyberbullying is even more toxic: it happens 24/7 with no escape, and it's significantly more public and indelible than bullying in the playground. Online platforms leave a permanent digital footprint, and like a virus, comments or photos, once shared, can be replicated and be impossible to control. The depth of pain caused by cyberbullying is reflected in the fact that **nearly one in four of those who've been cyber bullied have self-harmed in response to the bullying**. However, only one in ten of those being bullied has the confidence to delete the app they're being bullied on. [102]

Cyberbullying is, sadly, not something that just happens occasionally to other people. Some 51% of 12- to 15-year-olds who go online say that in the past 12 months they've seen *'something hateful on the internet directed at a particular group of people'.* [103] Many young people have reported that they feel stupid, ugly or useless because of something that's been said to them online. Cyberbullying is an upsetting and horrible experience. If it's happening to you, please don't suffer in silence. There are ways to get help.

HOW TO FIND HELP IF YOU'RE BEING CYBERBULLIED:

- Tell a trusted adult. It may feel scary, but they will want to know, and they can help.
- At the very least, try to ignore the message(s). Bullies are often looking for a response.
- Add comment restrictions to your account, and don't be afraid to block and report people if they're bullying you. Blocking people or deleting an app isn't a sign of weakness but puts you back in control.
- Screenshot messages so that you have evidence of the bullying if required.
- Try to involve your school, especially if it happens during school time.
- Seek help from professional organisations - for example, Childline and the NSPCC. [104]

SEXTING

At a local school disco, phone numbers were shared, and not long after, some girls got requests to send naked photos of themselves. The sender threatened that he would kill himself if he didn't get the images. In fear, several girls sent explicit pictures of themselves, which they later deeply regretted. Sensibly, they then shared what had happened with a parent and the school. The police became involved and reprimanded the boy in question as a reminder that this sort of behaviour is entirely unacceptable, deeply damaging and against the law.

Sexting is the sharing of explicit photos via smartphones and social media. In 2017 a survey by Ditch the Label (an anti-bullying charity) found that up to one in three teenagers had sent nude pictures of themselves online. [105] However, the greatest danger isn't the consensual sending of an image to a boyfriend or girlfriend. The greatest risk is of sending it inadvertently to a predatory stranger or having it shared without your consent. **A quarter of teenagers who've sent an explicit photo have had it forwarded without their consent.** [106] This can be extremely humiliating. Pictures can also end up on a revenge porn website for all to see (revenge porn is the posting of explicit photos on online porn sites without consent in order to humiliate and upset the person involved). In addition, a growing number of self-generated images (pictures taken by the young person themselves) are being used on child abuse sites. These include images that were originally shared consensually and are the result of peer-to-peer grooming. And there's the growing issue of AI-generated images and fake porn. In these cases, the original image is AI generated, but it's almost impossible to distinguish from a real photo or video and can be equally distressing for the victim.

Remember, once an image is shared, you lose control of how it's used. This can lead to bullying, blackmail, online grooming and abuse. Also, the digital footprint of these images is permanent. It's almost impossible to get the image back or get it taken down from websites. Sites like Snapchat can encourage this image-sharing behaviour because the photos auto-delete after being seen. You may, therefore, feel these images are safe from replication. However, a simple screenshot by the recipient makes them permanent (or you can download software that, unbeknown to the sender, automatically downloads and stores all snaps).

There can be intense pressure to share photos: the fear of being dumped, or the desire to be liked and fit in. It's important to remember that it's illegal to send, share or hold indecent photos of anyone under the age of 18.

WHERE TO GET HELP:

- We all make mistakes. If you ever find yourself in trouble and an image gets out, it's important to tell someone and seek help.
- You can reach out to various sources for support, including ChildLine, friends, parents, teachers, tutors and counsellors.
- Reporting the problem is crucial. You can report to CEOP (Child Exploitation and Online Protection) and receive assistance and guidance from a child protection officer.

GROOMING

Phoebe was very creative and loved to dance. TikTok seemed to be the perfect platform for her to express her creativity. Her profile was public, and she soon amassed hundreds of followers. One follower showed particular interest in her dances. Over time he befriended her online and persuaded her to meet him in person in an isolated spot. He posed as a 16-year-old local schoolboy. Luckily for Phoebe, she confided her plans to two friends, who persuaded her not to go. When she pulled out of the meet-up, he flooded her with indecent photos and threatened her. He certainly was not a 16-year-old schoolboy but an experienced predator looking for a vulnerable young girl. Whilst this episode was damaging and upsetting, Phoebe escaped relatively unscathed. Many others haven't.

Online grooming is when someone befriends a young person online and builds up their trust in order to exploit them and cause them harm. The harm caused by grooming can be sexual abuse (both in-person and online), or exploitation to get sexually explicit images and videos of the child. [107] In 2020, police in England and Wales had recorded over 10,000 online grooming offences on social media over the past two and a half years. Where the method was recorded, more than half took place on a Facebook-owned app (including Facebook, Instagram and WhatsApp). [108]

Online groomers lure young people through ever-increasingly complex methods of deception and deceit. They're very skilled at what they do and often befriend a child by appearing to have the same hobbies and interests. They look for vulnerable children with specific characteristics and make them feel special and understood. Using fake accounts and photos, they may also appear to be the same age as the child. However, not all groomers will choose to mask their age or gender. Some groomers may impersonate an aspirational figure such as a modelling scout, sports coach, celebrity or influencer. Others may use their age and experience to develop a mentor-type relationship with their victim.

WAYS TO STAY SAFE FROM GROOMING: [109]

- Never share your real name, age, address or school with a stranger online.
- Never give away information that would help them identify you or where you live; for example, your school logo on your jumper.
- Be wary of people you meet online who seem to show an unusual interest in you, offer you free stuff, or share all the same hobbies and interests.
- Tell a trusted adult straight away if an online friend wants to meet you in person or threatens you.
- Think about having a private account.
- Turn off GPS tracking and never disclose your location.
- Remember, not everyone online is who they say they are.
- **Report the problem:** You can report to CEOP and get help and advice from a child protection officer.

CATFISHING

Catfishing is the use of a fake online identity to pretend to be someone you're not for personal gain in a relationship. The term 'catfish' was coined from a 2010 US documentary about a man being deceived by a woman with a fake Facebook profile. If you think about it, in today's technological age it's not even a very hard thing to do. You can create a completely fake life online with photos, stories and images stolen from someone else. There are different reasons people catfish: some are lonely and looking for connections, while others are trying to scam their victims for money or explicit photos.

How many of us reading this already have our cloned identities floating around cyberspace? How can we be sure our photos aren't already in circulation and fake profiles set up in our names? It's a scary thought. False identities are easy to assume online, and the experienced 'catfisher' can be incredibly convincing. Also, how do we know who anyone really is online if we haven't met them in person or know of them via a personal connection? The important message is not to live in fear but to take the necessary precautions. Carefully check out the profiles of new friends online and verify their basic details. Catfishers will never agree to meet in person or even chat via video call.

SIGNS TO LOOK OUT FOR:

- New profile on social media
- Elaborate profile with either stolen or professional picture
- No mutual friends and few followers online
- Little or no online presence
- They ask you a lot of questions but give very little information away about themselves
- They have elaborate reasons why they can't meet in person or video call
- They give convincing (but highly unlikely) reasons they need large sums of money

WHAT TO DO IF YOU SUSPECT YOU'RE BEING CATFISHED:

- If you suspect that they've stolen photos, you can use Google Reverse Image Search to find similar pictures and where they came from. To use this, simply click on the camera icon on Google Images and upload the picture, or paste a picture's URL.
- It sounds obvious, but never send money to someone you've only met online, and the same goes for explicit photos.
- Report and block the person on your social media apps.
- If a crime has been committed, report it to the police.
- Tell your parents and/or a trusted adult.

TROLLING

A troll is someone who shares hate online with the intent of causing offence and disrupting online communities. Trolls often hide behind anonymous or fake accounts and say things they wouldn't say face to face or in real life. It's hard to know why trolls troll, but they may be seeking attention or revenge, or be motivated by their ideology. Trolls thrive on eliciting a response from those they attack. They may feel emboldened to say hurtful things online as there's little risk of real-world consequences. They may aim to cause maximal hurt by repeatedly targeting the same individual or group from a number of fake accounts. Trolls may make malicious comments about an individual's race, gender, looks or views.

Not all hurtful comments online are actually trolling. We can all express our opinions online, but it's important to think about the impact these comments will have on others. It's incredibly easy to post something offensive in the spur of the moment or without really thinking. You don't want to ruin someone else's day because you lost control in the heat of the moment.

Trolling is on the increase, as is the impact it's having on individuals. The internet is incredibly hard to police and trolling is a very difficult practice to stop. It can cause great hurt to those involved, and damage their well-being and self-esteem (especially if attacks are specifically targeted at individual characteristics).

SIGNS OF TROLLING:

- You're receiving targeted abusive comments online from accounts you don't know.
- The comments are generated from anonymous or fake accounts with no photos or names.
- You receive multiple personalised comments that are upsetting or inflammatory.
- The comments are targeted at a particular community you're part of, view you hold or individual physical characteristics.

WHAT TO DO IF YOU'RE BEING TROLLED:

- **Don't engage with the troll(s).** They're literally *waiting* for you to respond. One of the main reasons people troll is because they enjoy the responses they receive. The best thing you can do (however hard) is to ignore them.
- **Block and report.** Most social media apps have a system to block accounts and report abuse. Don't be afraid to block any account that posts upsetting things about you online and delete their comments.
- **Document evidence.** You can screenshot the comments or your feed as evidence, which may be needed later if the police become involved.
- **Change your security settings.** Make sure your social media accounts are secure. Consider changing your passwords and setting up two-factor authentication. Also consider changing your accounts to private, which will give trolls much less access to you.
- **Seek support.** If you're being trolled online, don't suffer in silence. Tell your parents or a trusted adult and they can help you find a way forward. Remember, the troll wants to isolate you - they want you to feel bad and suffer alone. Don't allow them this victory.

TOP TIPS FOR BEING RESPONSIBLE ONLINE:

- **Think before you post.** Let the moment pass and then decide if this is a suitable comment to post.
- **Would you say it in person?** It's much easier to say things online than in person, but the words you post can be just as hurtful and impact your friendships and relationships. Try to only post things online that you would say to a person's face.
- **How will it make the other person feel?** It's important to imagine what impact your post will have on someone else. Try to only post things that are positive and kind rather than cruel and hurtful. No one likes receiving negative comments, so try not to be the source of other people's pain.
- **Step away from online arguments.** It's easy to get sucked into other people's arguments online. Debates can get heated and other people may express opinions that are hurtful or completely illogical to you. However, getting involved with destructive online debates is rarely productive and can quickly become abusive. It's safer to step away and save the debate for the dinner table or a safer and less polarised environment.

RESOURCES

The following organisations provide information and support that may help you. Some of the info is aimed at parents, but you may still find it useful. Some sites are for under-18s, while others are aimed at students and young adults. Please note that specific web addresses change from time to time, so you may need to find the information by searching for an organisation's homepage.

ORGANISATIONS THAT OFFER ADVICE OR SUPPORT

BEAT, THE UK'S EATING DISORDER CHARITY

www.beateatingdisorders.org.uk

BEAT is a UK-based charity providing support, information and advocacy for individuals affected by eating disorders and their families.

CHILD EXPLOITATION AND ONLINE PROTECTION (CEOP)

www.ceop.police.uk/Safety-Centre

This site is where you can report online sexual abuse or the way someone has been communicating with you online.

CHILDLINE

www.childline.org.uk or call **0800 1111** (free)

Confidential advice for anyone aged 18 or younger. You can contact Childline 24 hours a day, 7 days a week, and talk to them about anything.

CHILDNET

www.childnet.com

Childnet offers valuable information and guidance on various essential online-safety topics, assisting users in navigating the digital world securely.

GAME QUITTERS

https://gamequitters.com

Free advice and support for overcoming gaming disorder including articles, video clips and a link to a paid game-addiction programme.

GET SAFE ONLINE

www.getsafeonline.org

Practical advice on digital safety.

MIND

www.mind.org.uk

Mind offers invaluable support by providing comprehensive information and resources to help individuals navigate and cope with mental health challenges.

NHS

www.nhs.uk

A complete guide to conditions, symptoms and treatments, including what to do and when to get help.

NIGHTLINE

www.nightline.ac.uk

Nightline is a unique listening service offered to students nationwide, providing confidential support during nighttime hours.

SHOUT

https://giveusashout.org or text **85258** (free)

A free confidential support service via text message. You can text any time, day or night, on 85258.

YOUTHSCAPE

www.youthscape.co.uk/mentalhealthhub

Youthscape's Mental Health Hub website is a valuable resource providing mental health resources and guidance tailored for young people.

YOUNG MINDS

www.youngminds.org.uk

Young Minds provides comprehensive resources and support for young people struggling with mental health, offering information, advice and signposting for those in need.

HELP WITH REDUCING PORNOGRAPHY USE

REWARD FOUNDATION

https://rewardfoundation.org

The Reward Foundation is a charity focused on providing relationship and sex education to promote healthy behaviours and attitudes.

NAKED TRUTH PROJECT

https://nakedtruthproject.com

The Naked Truth Project is dedicated to transforming lives by raising awareness, providing education and offering recovery programmes focused on issues related to sexual exploitation and pornography.

SUICIDE PREVENTION

SAMARITANS

www.samaritans.org or call **116 123** (free)

For anyone in crisis. Support and advice 24 hours a day, 7 days a week.

PAPYRUS

www.papyrus-uk.org or call **0800 068 4141** (free)

Confidential suicide-prevention advice for young people, open 24/7.

COGNITIVE BEHAVIOURAL THERAPY (CBT)

MOODGYM

https://moodgym.com.au

Moodgym is similar to an interactive self-help book. This low-cost online programme helps you to learn and practise skills to prevent and manage symptoms of depression and anxiety.

NHS

www.nhs.uk/service-search/mental-health/find-an-NHS-talking-therapies-service

You can put your details into this NHS website to find your local CBT provider, or contact your GP surgery for the details. You can then use the link to self-refer online for free CBT and other talking therapies available on the NHS.

SILVERCLOUD

www.silvercloudhealth.com/uk

Ask your GP or university for access to this online mental-health platform.

ACKNOWLEDGEMENTS

Thank you to all my friends and family for listening and supporting me through hours of my endless talk about phones, PAPAYA, book edits, tech addiction, mental health, and more.

A special thanks to Hugh for the endless pillow talk dominated by this topic, for his numerous reads and rereads of this book, for being my sounding board, and for his enduring emotional support. I love you.

To my wonderful children, Isabelle, Beth, and Theo: thank you for being amazing in every way and for bearing with my unwavering mission to get kids off their devices.

To my PAPAYA trustees, past (Victoria Bowden and Nicky Kooner) and present (Joe Watson, Alice Bond, and Jo Crow), for their support and dedication to the cause. A special thank you to John Beckwith for helping get PAPAYA up and running again after the pandemic and for handling all the admin jobs I dislike.

To Fritha Saunders for editing with such insight, to Charlie Wilson for going above and beyond with the copy editing, and to Michelle Bullock for proofreading and catching my final dyslexic mistakes.

Thank you, Miguel Fernandez, for the beautiful illustrations and for leading the way in using art to highlight the impact of technology on young people.

And to Collette Sadler for designing the book and turning my words into something beautiful.

Thank you, Clare Fernyhough and Daisy Greenwell, for starting Smartphone Free Childhood and pioneering a wave of change in the UK. Hopefully, the next generation won't need this book, thanks to you.

Thank you to Katherine Hill and Dr Becky Foljambe for your professional reading of the book, your insightful feedback, and your comments for the cover.

To my 'giggling girls' (Rachel Smith, Dominique Knight, and Jo Crow) for their unwavering support and prosecco drinking.

To my fantastic prayer support team (Becka Huckett, Sarah Douglas, Alice Bond, and Joe Watson).

To my neighbours, Jonathan and Jessica Dimbleby, for their wonderful friendship and for the words by Jonathan.

Thank you, Mum and Dad, Pam and Tony, for being wonderful parents and grandparents, and for all the happy times we've shared together.

To all the children who have come to our PAPAYA workshops and all my patients who have let me help them on their path to emotional wellness and achieving a healthy balance with technology: it is, and always will be, a privilege to hear your stories and to help you find your way.

And finally, thank you to all my beautiful readers. I hope you are finding your 'Healthy Selfie'.

10% of the profit will be shared between PAPAYA, Smartphone Free Childhood, and Save the Children.

[1] Mills, J. S., Musto, S., Williams, L. et al. (2018). 'Selfie' harm: Effects on mood and body image in young women. Body Image, 27, 86–92. https://doi.org/10.1016/j.bodyim.2018.08.007.

[2] Crenna-Jennings, W. (2021). Young people's mental and emotional health: Trajectories and drivers in childhood and adolescence. Education Policy Institute. https://dera.ioe.ac.uk/id/eprint/37301.

[3] Peden, A. R., Hall, L. A., Rayens, M. K. et al. (2000). Negative thinking mediates the effect of self-esteem on depressive symptoms in college women. Nursing Research, 49(4), 201-207. https://pubmed.ncbi.nlm.nih.gov/10929691.

[4] Eger, E. E. (2020). The Gift. Scribner.

[5] Moore, C. (2019, 2 June). How to practice self-compassion: 8 techniques and tips. PositivePsychology.com. https://positivepsychology.com/how-to-practice-self-compassion.

[6] Neff, K. D., Hsieh, Y.-P. & Dejitterat, K. (2005). Self-compassion, achievement goals, and coping with academic failure. Self and Identity, 4(3), 263–287. https://doi.org/10.1080/13576500444000317.

[7] Brown, B. (2021). Atlas of the Heart. Random House.

[8] Eger, E. E. (2020).

[9] Yahoo! (n.d.). Teen left bedridden by Snapchat addiction. Yahoo! Style. https://uk.yahoo.com/style/teen-left-bedridden-snapchat-addiction-2-093621197.html.

[10] Ofcom (2020, 4 February). Parents' rising concern over children online. https://www.ofcom.org.uk/about-ofcom/latest/media/media-releases/2020/rising-concern-over-children-online.

[11] Ditch the Label (2020, 8 October). The Annual Bullying Survey 2017. https://mx.ditchthelabel.org/research-papers/the-annual-bullying-survey-2017.

[12] Peterson, S. J., Van Tongeren, D. R., Womack, S. D. et al. The benefits of self-forgiveness on mental health: Evidence from correlational and experimental research. The Journal of Positive Psychology, 12(2), 159-168. https://doi.org/10.1080/17439760.2016.1163407.

[13] Cherry, K. (n.d.). How to forgive yourself. Verywell Mind. https://www.verywellmind.com/how-to-forgive-yourself-4583819.

[14] BBC News (2022, 9 April). Gen Z calling for more honesty on social media, experts say. https://www.bbc.co.uk/news/uk-england-somerset-60022871.

[15] Thai, H., Davis, C. G., Mahboob, W. et al. (2023). Reducing social media use improves appearance and weight esteem in youth with emotional distress. Psychology of Popular Media. https://doi.org/10.1037/ppm0000460.

[16] Baumeister, R. F., Campbell, J. D., Krueger, J. I. et al. (2003). Does high self-esteem cause better performance, interpersonal success, happiness, or healthier lifestyles? Psychological Science in the Public Interest, 4(1), 1–44. https://doi.org/10.1111/1529-1006.01431.

[17] Peden, A. R., Hall, L. A., Rayens, M. K. et al. (2000).

[18] Kelly, R. (2015). Thrive. Rob Kelly Publishing.

[19] Twenge, J. M. (2017, September). Have smartphones destroyed a generation? The Atlantic. https://www.theatlantic.com/magazine/archive/2017/09/has-the-smartphone-destroyed-a-generation/534198.

[20] Burton, C. M. & King, L. A. (2004). The health benefits of writing about intensely positive experiences. Journal of Research in Personality, 38(2), 150-163. https://doi.org/10.1016/s0092-6566(03)00058-8.

[21] Kelly, R. (2015).

[22] Taylor, C., Lyubomirsky, S. & Stein, M. B. (2017). Upregulating the positive affect system in anxiety and depression: Outcomes of a positive activity intervention. Depression and Anxiety, 34(3), 267-280. https://doi.org/10.1002/da.22593.

[23] Cregg, D. R. & Cheavens, J. S. (2021). Gratitude interventions: Effective self-help? A meta-analysis of the impact on symptoms of depression and anxiety. Journal of Happiness Studies, 22, 413–445. https://doi.org/10.1007/s10902-020-00236-6.

[24] Mackesy, C. (2019). The Boy, the Mole, the Fox and the Horse. HarperCollins.

[25] Gawdat, M. (2017). Solve for Happy. Boxtree.

[26] Thompson, D. & Vailes, F. (2019). How to Grow a Grown Up. Random House.

[27] Kelly, R. (2013). Thrive for Teenagers. Rob Kelly Publishing.

[28] Haferkamp, N. & Krämer, N. C. (2011). Social comparison 2.0: Examining the effects online profiles on social-networking sites. Cyberpsychology, Behavior, and Social Networking, 14(5), 309-314. https://doi.org/10.1089/cyber.2010.0120.

[29] Kondo, M. (2014). The Life-Changing Magic of Tidying Up. Ten Speed Press.

[30] Vandenbosch, L., Fardouly, J. & Tiggemann, M. (2022). Social media and body image: Recent trends and future directions. Current Opinion in Psychology, 45, 101289. https://doi.org/10.1016/j.copsyc.2021.12.002

[31] Hemmings, J. (ed.) (2018). How Psychology Works. DK.

[32] Das, J. K., Salam, R. A., Lassi, Z. S. et al. (2016). Interventions for adolescent mental health: An overview of systematic reviews. The Journal of Adolescent Health: Official Publication of the Society for Adolescent Medicine, 59(4S), S49-S60. https://doi.org/10.1016/j.jadohealth.2016.06.020.

[33] NHS. (2019, 16 July). Cognitive behavioural therapy (CBT). https://www.nhs.uk/mental-health/talking-therapies-medicine-treatments/talking-therapies-and-counselling/cognitive-behavioural-therapy-cbt/overview.

[34] Eger, E. E. (2020).

[35] Neff, K. D., Kirkpatrick, K. L. & Rude, S. S. (2007).

[36] Dweck, C. (2017). Mindset. Robinson.

[37] Dweck, C. (2017).

[38] Elliot-Moskwa, E. (2022). The Growth Mindset Workbook. New Harbinger Publications.

[39] Ofcom (n.d.). Children and parents: Media use and attitudes report. https://www.ofcom.org.uk/__data/assets/pdf_file/0020/108182/children-parents-media-use-attitudes-2017.pdf.

[40] Grylls, B. (2011). Facing Up. Macmillan.

[41] Elliot-Moskwa, E. (2022).

[42] Lancer, N., Clutterbuck D. & Megginson, D. (2016). Techniques for Coaching and Mentoring. Routledge.

[43] Nagoski, E. & Nagoski, A. (2019). Burnout. Random House.

[44] Davis, T. (n.d.). Core values: List, examples, and exercises. The Berkeley Well-Being Institute. https://www.berkeleywellbeing.com/core-values.html.

[45] Davis, T. (n.d.).

[46] BBC (2018, 1 October). 16-24 year olds are the loneliest age group according to new BBC Radio 4 survey. https://www.bbc.co.uk/mediacentre/latestnews/2018/loneliest-age-group-radio-4.

[47] Alsarrani, A., Hunter, R. F., Dunne, L. et al. (2022). Association between friendship quality and subjective wellbeing among adolescents: A systematic review. BMC Public Health, 22(1), 2420. https://doi.org/10.1186/s12889-022-14776-4.

[48] Dignify (n.d.). What young people are telling us. https://dignify.org.

[49] Wain, P. (2023, 9 May). Children's commissioner: Pornography affecting 8-year-olds' behaviour. BBC News. https://www.bbc.co.uk/news/technology-65534354.

[50] Wright, P. J., Bridges, A. J., Sun, C. et al. (2018). Personal pornography viewing and sexual satisfaction: A quadratic analysis. Journal of Sex and Marital Therapy, 44(3): 308-315. https://pubmed.ncbi.nlm.nih.gov/28885897.

[51] Voon, V., Mole, T. B., Banca, P. et al. (2014, 11 July). Neural correlates of sexual cue reactivity in individuals with and without compulsive sexual behaviours. PLOS ONE. https://journals.plos.org/plosone/article?id=10.1371%2Fjournal.pone.0102419.

[52] September 1, 2014 issue of Jama Psychiatry. September 1, 2014 Issue of JAMA Psychiatry | JAMA Network. (n.d.). https://jamanetwork.com/journals/jamapsychiatry/issue/71/9.

[53] Boyle, S. (2022, 28 August). How the king of toxic masculinity corrupted a generation: Andrew Tate's diatribes against women saw him get more Google hits than Donald Trump last month - until he was banned by social media giants. Daily Mail Online. https://www.dailymail.co.uk/tvshowbiz/article-11154837/How-king-toxic-masculinity-corrupted-generation.html.

[54] Borrud, G. & Dillon, C. (2023, 18 September). Toxic masculinity expert: 'Andrew Tate is a disaster'. DW.com. https://www.dw.com/en/toxic-masculinity-expert-andrew-tate-is-a-disaster/a-66799601.

[55] Progressive Masculinity (n.d.). http://progressivemasculinity.co.uk.

[56] Schoen, M. (2014). Your Survival Instinct Is Killing You. Penguin.

[57] Nagoski, E. & Nagoski, A. (2019).

[58] Nagoski, E. & Nagoski, A. (2019).

[59] Ramos-Sanchez, C. P., Schuch, F. B., Seedat, S. et al. (2021). The anxiolytic effects of exercise for people with anxiety and related disorders: An update of the available meta-analytic evidence. Psychiatry Research, 302, 114046. https://doi.org/10.1016/j.psychres.2021.114046.

[60] Perciavalle, V., Blandini, M., Fecarotta, P. et al. (2017). The role of deep breathing on stress. Neurological Sciences, 38(3), 451–458. https://doi.org/10.1007/s10072-016-2790-8.

[61] Chatterjee, R. (2017). The Four Pillar Plan. Penguin Life.

[62] Manninen, S., Tuominen, L., Dunbar, R. et al. (2017). Social laughter triggers endogenous opioid release in humans. Journal of Neuroscience, 37(25), 6125–6131. https://doi.org/10.1523/jneurosci.0688-16.2017.

[63] Manninen, S., Tuominen, L., Dunbar, R. et al. (2017).

[64] Chatterjee, R. (2022, 1 May). The secret to solving the stress cycle with Drs Emily and Amelia Nagoski. DrChatterjee.com. https://drchatterjee.com/the-secret-to-solving-the-stress-cycle-with-drs-emily-and-amelia-nagoski.

[65] Kaimal, G., Ray, K. & Muniz, J. (2016). Reduction of cortisol levels and participants' responses following art making. Art Therapy, 33(2), 74–80. https://doi.org/10.1080/07421656.2016.1166832.

[66] Childwise (n.d.). Childhood 2020: New independent report. http://www.childwise.co.uk/uploads/3/1/6/5/31656353/childwise_press_release_-_monitor_2020_-_immediate_release.pdf.

[67] Burnett, D. (2019). Why Your Parents Are Driving You Up the Wall and What You Can Do About It. Puffin.

[68] Chatterjee, R. (2017).

[69] Woods, H. C. & Scott, H. (2016). #Sleepyteens: Social media use in adolescence is associated with poor sleep quality, anxiety, depression and low self-esteem. Journal of Adolescence, 51, 41–49. https://doi.org/10.1016/j.adolescence.2016.05.008.

[70] Holland and Barrett (n.d.). Health Hub Home. http://www.hollandandbarrett.com/the-health-hub.

[71] Holland and Barrett (n.d.).

[72] Ganson, K. T., Hallward, L., Rodgers, R. F. et al. (2023). Contemporary screen use and symptoms of muscle dysmorphia among a national sample of Canadian adolescents and young adults. Eating and Weight Disorders, 28(1): 10. https://www.ncbi.nlm.nih.gov/pmc/articles/PMC9930713.

[73] Crenna-Jennings, W. (2021).

[74] All on the Board (2020, 10 October). Today is #WorldMentalHealthDay... Twitter. https://twitter.com/allontheboard/status/1314837829046931456?lang=en.

[75] BBC (n.d.). What's it like to be a teenager? (And some handy advice on how to survive). BBC Bitesize. https://www.bbc.co.uk/bitesize/articles/zg88mbk.

[76] Center for Humane Technology. (n.d.). Together we can align technology with humanity's best interests. https://www.humanetech.com.

[77] Independent Online (2022, 30 September). Molly Russell inquest – coroner's conclusion in full. https://www.independent.co.uk/news/uk/molly-russell-inquest-coroner-s-conclusion-in-full-b2183287.html.

[78] Crenna-Jennings, W. (2021).

[79] Sahu, M., Gandhi, S. & Sharma, M. K. (2019). Mobile phone addiction among children and adolescents: A systematic review. Journal of Addictions Nursing, 30(4): 261–268. https://pubmed.ncbi.nlm.nih.gov/31800517.

[80] Gomez, S. (2023, February 21). Phone addiction: Warning signs and treatment. Addiction Center. https://www.addictioncenter.com/drugs/phone-addiction.

[81] Hassan, S. (2022, 5 May). How to free our minds – with cult deprogramming expert Dr Steven Hassan. Your Undivided Attention, Apple Podcasts. https://podcasts.apple.com/us/podcast/how-to-free-our-minds-with-cult-deprogramming-expert/id1460030305?i=1000559682409.

[82] Mark, G., Daniela, G. & Klocke, U. (2008). The cost of interrupted work: More speed and stress. CHI '08 Proceedings of the SIGCHI Conference on Human Factors in Computing Systems, April, 107–110.

[83] Felisoni, D. D. & Godoi, A. S. (2018). Cell phone usage and academic performance. Computers and Education, 117(C), 175–187. https://dl.acm.org/doi/10.1016/j.compedu.2017.10.006.

[84] Firstpost (2013, 11 February). Smartphone users check their devices 150 times a day, says study. https://www.firstpost.com/tech/news-analysis/smartphone-users-check-their-devices-150-times-a-day-says-study-2-3619465.html.

[85] García, H. & Miralles, F. (2017). Ikigai: The Japanese secret to a long and happy life. Hutchinson.

[86] Ellwood, B. (2022, 25 January). Teens who are 'addicted' to TikTok experience worse depression and anxiety, and in turn, reduced working memory capacity. PsyPost. https://www.psypost.org/2022/01/teens-who-are-addicted-to-tiktok-experience-worse-depression-and-anxiety-and-in-turn-reduced-working-memory-capacity-62416.

[87] Wacks, Y. & Weinstein, A. M. (2021, 28 May). Excessive smartphone use is associated with health problems in adolescents and young adults. Frontiers in Psychiatry. https://www.frontiersin.org/articles/10.3389/fpsyt.2021.669042/full.

[88] UCL (2017, 20 September). One in four girls is depressed at age 14, new study reveals. IOE Faculty of Education and Society. https://www.ucl.ac.uk/ioe/news/2017/sep/one-four-girls-depressed-age-14-new-study-reveals.

[89] Crenna-Jennings, W. (2021).

[90] NHS. (n.d.). NHS choices. https://digital.nhs.uk/data-and-information/publications/statistical/mental-health-of-children-and-young-people-in-england/2022-follow-up-to-the-2017-survey.

[91] Weale, S. (2022, 7 February). Pupils in England reluctant to return to school after lockdown, says report. Guardian. https://www.theguardian.com/education/2022/feb/07/pupils-in-england-reluctant-to-return-to-school-after-lockdown-says-report.

[92] World Health Organization (2020, 22 October). Addictive behaviours: Gaming disorder. Who.int. https://www.who.int/news-room/questions-and-answers/item/addictive-behaviours-gaming-disorder

[93] Issuesonline.co.uk (2022). Skin gambling: teenage Britain's secret habit. https://www.issuesonline.co.uk/articles/skin-gambling-teenage-britains-secret-habit.

[94] Stevens, M. W. R., Dorstyn, D., Delfabbro, P. H. et al. (2021, June). Global prevalence of gaming disorder: A systematic review and meta-analysis. Australian and New Zealand Journal of Psychiatry, 55(6): 553–568. https://pubmed.ncbi.nlm.nih.gov/33028074.

[95] Przybylski, A., Weinstein, N. & Murayama, K. (2017). Internet gaming disorder: Investigating the Clinical relevance of a new phenomenon. American Journal of Psychiatry, 174(3), 230–236. https://doi.org/10.1176/appi.ajp.2016.16020224.

[96] Bliss, D. (2020, 2 March). Gaming disorder: The rise of a 21st century epidemic. National Geographic. https://www.nationalgeographic.co.uk/science-and-technology/2020/02/gaming-disorder-rise-of-21st-century-epidemic.

[97] Game Quitters (2021, 26 July). Ready to overcome your video game addiction? https://gamequitters.com.

[98] Definition from the Cambridge Dictionary.

[99] Thai, H., Davis, C. G., Mahboob, W. et al. (2023).

[100] Royal College of Paediatrics and Child Health (n.d.). The health impacts of screen time – a guide for clinicians and parents. https://www.rcpch.ac.uk/resources/health-impacts-screen-time-guide-clinicians-parents.

[101] Ditch the Label (2022). The Annual Bullying Survey 2017. http://ABS_2017_1_ae04a7734b.pdf (dtl-beta-website-assets.s3.amazonaws.com)

[102] Ditch the Label (2022).

[103] Ofcom (2022, 4 February). Parents' rising concern over children online. https://www.ofcom.org.uk/about-ofcom/latest/media/media-releases/2020/rising-concern-over-children-online.

[104] NSPCC (n.d.). Bullying and cyberbullying. https://www.nspcc.org.uk/what-is-child-abuse/types-of-abuse/bullying-and-cyberbullying.

[105] Ditch the Label (2022).

[106] Ditch the Label (2022).

[107] Childnet (2022). Online grooming. https://www.childnet.com/help-and-advice/online-grooming.

[108] BBC (2020, 29 May). Facebook dominates cases of recorded social media grooming. BBC News. https://www.bbc.com/news/technology-52841358. 109 Childnet (2022).

[109] Childnet (2022)

Author

Dr Susie Davies is a General Practitioner based in inner-city Bristol. Born in Oxford and raised in Somerset, she qualified as a GP in 2013. Her work with students ignited a passion for young people's mental health and the impact of technology. In 2018, she founded the charity PAPAYA, dedicated to helping families achieve a positive balance with technology. Dr Davies conducts workshops in schools for both parents and students and is a frequent guest on radio and TV, where she discusses the effects of social media on young people. She is married to Hugh, and they have three adolescent children.

More information about her charitable work can be found on the website

papayaparents.com

@papaya_parents

@thehealthyselfiedr

Illustrator

Miguel Fernandez is the founder of Mafe Art Studio. Originally from Spain, Miguel is a former teacher dedicated to impacting the lives of young generations through his art. Motivated by a desire to make a tangible difference in children's mental health, Miguel transitioned from the classroom to the canvas. His mission revolves around using art as a catalyst for change, particularly in addressing the impact of technology on children.

You can find out more about Miguel and his powerful work on his website

mafeartstudio.com

@mafe.artstudio